Poland's Jump to the Market Economy

The Lionel Robbins Lectures

Poland's Jump to the Market Economy

Jeffrey Sachs

The MIT Press
Cambridge, Massachusetts
London, England

Second MIT Press paperback edition, 1999

This book was set in Palatino by .eps Electronic Publishing Services and was printed and bound in the United States of America.

Library of Congress Cataloging-in-Publication Data

Sachs, Jeffrey.
   Poland's jump to the market economy : based on the Lionel Robbins
   Memorial lectures delivered at the London School of Economics,
   January 1991 / by Jeffrey Sachs.
      p.   cm. — (The Lionel Robbins Lectures.)
   Includes bibliographical references and index.
   ISBN 0-262-19312-4 (HB), 0-262-69174-4 (PB)
   1. Poland—Economic policy—1981–   2. Poland—Economic
   conditions—1980–   3. Capitalism—Poland. I. Title. II. Series.
   HC340.3.S21 1993   93-1738
   338.9438—dc20   CIP

To Walter Ehrlich,
whose lifetime of
commitment to freedom
and truth
deeply inspires all who
know him.

Contents

Series Foreword

The greatest challenge of this decade is how to change from communism to capitalism. It is a political and practical challenge, but it also requires the exercise of powerful economic reasoning.

Should prices be freed quickly or suddenly? How speedily should inflation be controlled? When should currencies become freely convertible? How should state property be privatized, and when? How can foreign finance help?

The world has been fortunate that one of its leading economists, Jeffrey Sachs, has devoted years of his life to thought and action on these questions. His conclusion, reached already by 1989, was that action should be as rapid as possible on all fronts. Since then he has applied his strong mind and tenacious powers of persuasion to developing appropriate plans of action in one country after another, as it abandoned communism. Rarely does an academic economist have such an immediate effect on world events.

Poland was the first country to change, and it became the testing ground for the big bang approach that Sachs advocated. He played a major role in the design and follow-through of the Balcerowicz Plan, which adopted this approach. To some people the approach was and remains anathema. But increasingly the evidence has been swinging in Sachs's favor. In Poland, the recession that followed the initial shock has bottomed out and strong growth has resumed. And other ex-communist countries that have not adopted shock therapy have done no better than Poland.

It does seem that the worst place to be is in-between capitalism and communism, and the best policy is to hasten through that phase as rapidly as possible. One can only admire the courage and intellectual clarity with which Jeffrey Sachs has stuck to that belief, in the face of often quite violent criticism.

The London School of Economics was delighted when he agreed to give the annual Lionel Robbins Memorial Lectures only one year after the Polish experiment began, and while the jury was still out. He has now updated the lectures but without, I am happy to say, having to alter any of the major arguments. His lectures focus on the Polish experience as an illustration of the fundamental principles he espouses.

This book is full of excellent economics and wise politics. It is beautifully written and a major contribution to the debate.

Richard Layard

Preface

It is almost exactly three years since the start of Poland's economic big bang and two years since I delivered the Lionel Robbins Memorial Lectures at the London School of Economics. That occasion provided an excellent opportunity for me to review the developments of the first year of Poland's reform and examine the basic propositions of radical reform in the face of a range of criticisms. I had expected to polish and publish the lectures soon afterward, but my work as economic advisor to the Polish government and the fast-moving events in Russia disrupted those plans. When I became economic advisor to the Russian government at the end of 1991, I put the lectures aside and could work on them only in fits and starts. Now, two years later, I am delighted to offer a revised and updated version of the lectures.

The intervening time has slightly changed the character of the lectures. Originally they were an elaboration of Poland's reform strategy, with only very early results yet evident. Now, in view of the delay, it is possible to assess the results of the reform more thoroughly. I am delighted, of course, that my early optimism concerning the reforms has been sustained by the events of the past two years. Although Poland's economic transformation is still far from complete and its young democracy is still fragile, almost all observers—most important, the Poles themselves—concur that the country is on the right track to democracy and a market economy tightly integrated with the rest of Europe.

Some of the economic accomplishments have been nothing less than remarkable. Poland's private sector is booming, with more than 700,000 new businesses registered in the two-and-one-half years since the start of the radical reforms. It is estimated that more than half of employment and GDP is now found in the private sector. Poland's industrial enterprises continue to make headway in new export markets in the West, with Poland's hard-currency-area exports rising from $8 billion in 1989 to around $14 billion in 1992. Western creditors have also wisely agreed to a two-stage cancellation of half of Poland's debts, thereby eliminating one of the great burdens on the economy and offering to Poland a true chance for a fresh start. Perhaps most important, the sense of panic that gripped the country in the early days of reform has dissipated. Confidence is returning. Most Poles report that their living standards have improved since the communist period.

Of course, as I shall describe, many key problems remain. Unemployment is high, though fortunately less severe than had been feared. Poland's budget remains in chronic deficit, threatening the hard-earned financial stability. Privatization of large-scale industrial enterprises remains slow, indeed nearly paralyzed, by the inability to achieve a political consensus on a program of mass privatization. And political institutions are still fragile, with twenty-nine political parties in the parliament, and the fragility that comes from a multiparty coalition government with no less than six parties!

Poland's economic reform approach has had enormous influence in the rest of the region. Czechoslovakia launched similar comprehensive reforms at the start of 1991, as did several other smaller countries. More dramatically, the first post-communist government of Boris Yeltsin in Russia launched a massive program of "economic shock therapy" at the start of 1992 clearly informed by the Polish experience. I have had the high honor of advising the Russian government on that program since its inception.

After three years of Poland's reforms and one year of Russia's reforms, I remain absolutely convinced in the potential for successful economic reforms throughout the region. Events have disproved the idea of a "Homo sovieticus" spoiled by decades of communism. As soon as economic and political liberties were established, new entrepreneurs surged forward with energy, determination, and capacity. Market activity has spread from the Elbe to Vladivostok, often even before legal norms have been put in place. It seems that the deadening decades of communism did not dull the acquisitive spirit, but rather sharpened it.

As I shall stress, therefore, the problem of reform is mostly political rather than social or even economic. Society accepts the need for change and is ready to slough off the brutality and artificiality of the communist system. This is especially the case when governments take care to provide targeted relief for the most vulnerable groups in society. Many of the economic problems also solve themselves: markets spring up as soon as central planning bureaucrats vacate the field.

The reformers must be able to maintain the direction of reform against the organized opposition of the old guard, the disorganized opposition of new populists who seek to gain power by playing on the public's fears, and the understandable anxieties of the general public. In the end, economic reform becomes a profound problem of leadership in a newly democratic setting, in which FDR's soothing words have never been more relevant, "Let me assert my firm belief that the only thing we have to fear is fear itself."

The West can play a crucial role in this difficult transition by helping to assuage the fears and thereby give the reforms time to take hold and become self-sustaining. As I shall stress in the case of Poland, the early Western assistance with a stabilization fund for the zloty and the two-stage cancellation of part of Poland's foreign debt have been extremely important in helping to keep the reform program on track and in giving Poland the chance for a true fresh start. The most important step remains, however. Poland's "return to Europe" will be secure only after it has firm commitments on a timetable for Poland's accession to the European Community.

The past four years have been a time of enormous personal challenge and fulfillment. I have been afforded the high honor and responsibility of advising several governments in Eastern Europe and the former Soviet Union on the design and implementation of economic reform programs. In 1989, I began assisting Poland's Solidarity movement on the day it was legalized, and I worked with some of the world's greatest democratic leaders—Lech Walesa, Bronislaw Geremek, Adam Michnik, Jacek Kuron—on the strategy for replacing the defunct communist system with a vigorous market economy. I then became an advisor to Poland's first noncommunist government and its remarkable first Deputy Prime Minister for Economy, Leszek Balcerowicz. Since then I have been honored to provide advice to governments in Slovenia, Russia, Estonia, Mongolia, and elsewhere.

Throughout this work, I have learned much more than I could have taught, and have built a debt of gratitude to countless talented and remarkable individuals. My greatest thanks go to my colleague David Lipton, who joined me in advisory work and study around the world during 1988 to 1992. In Russia, I have been extraordinarily privileged to work with Professor Anders Åslund of the Stockholm School of Economics, a Sovietologist and economist of unsurpassed scholarship, vision, and insight. Dozens of colleagues, students, and policymakers around the world with whom I have been privileged to work in recent years have contributed to the ideas of economic reform described in these lectures. I hope that they will understand my inability to mention them individually here, and accept my gratitude expressed collectively. Of course, many of their scholarly contributions are cited throughout the lectures.

Whatever I have been able to accomplish in recent years, I owe to my wife, Dr. Sonia Ehrlich, an accomplished physician, and mother and wife nonpareil, whose dedication to freedom in Eastern Europe and Russia has been both lodestar and sustenance during years of wearying travel and separation from family. To Sonia, and my children Lisa and Adam, my love and thanks for your patient understanding.

1   What Is To Be Done NOW?

I am particularly pleased to be at the London School of Economics because, as Professor Robbins and the esteemed faculty over the course of generations have proved, economics can be put to the service of mankind. I hope to demonstrate this in the very specific case of the transformation of Eastern Europe.

During the past three years, I have had the high personal honor of participating in the design and implementation of the economic reforms now under way in Poland, Russia, and other countries in the region. The reforms in Poland, introduced on January 1, 1990, have been especially far reaching, and have been widely recognized as a model for the reforms in other parts of Eastern Europe and the former Soviet Union. For reasons of personal experience, and because of the more general interest in Poland's reform strategy, I will focus mainly on Poland throughout these lectures. Where necessary, though, I will highlight important differences between Poland and other parts of Eastern Europe.

The title of my talk, "What Is to Be Done NOW?", is an obvious allusion to the question raised by Lenin at the beginning of the century, concerning the same region. What Lenin (1902) proposed as an answer—a dictatorship of the proletariat, led by an elite political party—resulted in one of the great disasters of the twentieth century. It may seem reckless, therefore, even to ask the same question. Indeed, some have claimed that any attempt to develop an economic blueprint for Eastern Europe's future development betrays the same mistake as Lenin's: the false, and dangerous, presumption that human society can be arranged, rather than simply allowed to evolve.

I think that this is wrong, a mistaken analogy to the recklessness and hubris of earlier revolutions. As I will explain, the current revolutions under way in Eastern Europe are not utopian, nor do they seek to impose a new social experiment, as was the case in Lenin's revolution. Today's revolutions are of a relentlessly pragmatic character. This makes all the difference.

Eastern Europeans are uninterested in the counsels of perfection that have caused so much trouble in the past. They are instead interested in putting in place the economic structures and strategies that have proved their worth in other countries, particularly in the neighboring countries of Western Europe. This interpretation, which I think is repeatedly confirmed in the statements and actions of Eastern European leaders and in the political choices of the general population, is the basis of the rest of my views on how to conduct the economic changes now under way. The motivation of the Eastern Europeans, in a simple yet compelling phrase, is "to return to Europe."

It has often been said that although hundreds of books offer advice on how to convert a capitalist economy to a socialist economy, starting with or preceding Lenin, no book describes how to go from socialism to capitalism. But this is not really true. The task ahead is not as mysterious nor as complex as it might seem; in fact, in many ways it is a well-trodden path. I do not agree with extravagant statements often made about the uniqueness of this situation, and therefore I do not feel that we are helpless in the face of the task ahead.

Although parts of the transformation represent uncharted territory (such as massive privatization of industry), many other aspects of Eastern Europe's reform tasks are quite familiar. Many other countries that were once cut off from the rest of the world by inward-looking, authoritarian regimes have successfully opened up and become integrated into the global mainstream economy. By doing so, they have tended to enjoy enormous increases in real income. In effect, by rejoining the rest of the global economy, they are able to import some of the prosperity from the rest of the world, usually through the importation of new technologies, organizational patterns, and finance. The prototypical case in Europe that I will refer to is that of Spain, which in many ways provides a kind of guidepost to the path that the countries of Eastern Europe should follow.

The hardest part of the transformation, in fact, will not be the economics at all, but the politics. The years ahead will provide innumerable challenges to the fragile democratic order now taking shape in Eastern Europe. After decades of stagnation, the Eastern economies must change fundamentally. But change, as Schumpeter reminded us, involves destruction as well as creation. There will be losers together with winners in Eastern Europe. In many cases, the winners will not be sure about their economic successes for years to come, well before politically important groups identify themselves as potential losers. The great political task is to follow the path of reform in the face of inevitable anxieties, vested interests fighting for the status quo, and demagogues ready to seek political power by playing on the public's fears.

Guideposts of Economic Reform

To make clear what I have in mind about the existence of clear guideposts for economic reforms, I would like to refer to the writing of a great scholar well known to you, Professor Ralf Dahrendorf (1990), who has written a fascinating book on the revolutions of 1989. I am going to focus on a point of disagreement—which is somewhat unfair because I agree with most of what he writes in his very thoughtful book. Let me quote what Dahrendorf says and then try to put it in some perspective in the context of Poland. He writes,

The common language we speak today is not the language of the West, now adopted by the East. It is an intrinsically universal language which belongs to nobody in particular and therefore to everybody. The countries of East-Central Europe have not shed their communist system in order to embrace the capitalist system—whatever that is. They have shed a closed system in order to create an open society. The open society, to be exact. For while there can be many systems, there is only one open society. If any creed has won in the events of last year, it is the idea that we are all embarked on a journey into an uncertain future and have to work by trial and error within institutions which make it possible to bring about change without bloodshed.

Although the book is mostly, and rightly, a celebration of freedom in the open society, I consider Professor Dahrendorf to be mistaken in his view that Eastern Europe did not shed the communist system to adopt capitalism. In my view, that is precisely what they have done, and all of their actions are directed toward this purpose. I should like to compare Dahrendorf's statement with one made in 1990 by Poland's chief negotiator with the European Community (EC). Concerning Poland's aim to negotiate an "association agreement" with the EC, as a stepping stone to full membership, he says,

The most important thing will be to harmonize economic policy and legislation. Poland will try to take an enormous step forward in coordinating its economic and monetary policy with that of the EEC, followed by policies on industry, customs duties, commerce, company law, conditions for residence, and the pursuit of economic activity—taxation, social matters, regional issues, environmental protection, agriculture, energy, scientific research, the protection of intellectual property. And that is still not everything. We know that joining the EEC means adopting about 7,000 legal regulations. At the present time we are at the process of translating the EEC code of preferential product listings. We also have asked the Community to produce a list of norms that we would introduce right away, because they are of exceptional importance.

That statement reflects the spirit of the economic reform program under way in Poland, and what *should* be the spirit of the economic reform programs in Eastern Europe generally. Poland's goal is to be like the states of the European Community. Although there are many submodels within Western Europe, with distinct versions of the modern welfare state, the Western European economies share a common core of capitalist institutions. It is that common core that should be the aim of the Eastern European reforms. The finer points of choosing between different submodels—the Scandinavian social welfare state, Thatcherism, the German social market—can be put off until later, once the core institutions are firmly in place.[1]

Thus economic harmonization with Western Europe and eventual membership in the European Community are fundamental goals of the Eastern European countries—and they determine the fundamental strategy guiding the reform effort. Pursuing this basic strategy will make success possible, just as it led to an economic flowering in Spain after Spain abandoned its autarkic policies at the end of the 1950s. If instead the philosophy were one of open experimentation, I doubt that the transformation would be possible at all, at least without costly and dangerous wrong turns. As I shall explain, there are several risks that the whole reform effort can still get blown off course. The real reason for optimism lies in the fact that the endpoint is so clearly discerned.

If Eastern Europe is indeed trying to return to Western Europe, an obvious implication is that success in the economic transformation will depend not only on the East, but quite fundamentally on the West as well. It will take actions on both sides for Eastern Europe to "return to Europe." Therein lies a whole range of problems related to the willingness of Western Europe to act with the vision necessary to open its borders—not only to industrial goods but also to agriculture, and not only to commodities but also to people from the East—so that all of Europe can be a unified and integrated region. Thus the West cannot escape responsibility for the changes ahead. In the absence of a generous and visionary approach by the West, however, it will prove impossible to achieve success in the reforms—no matter how resolute Eastern Europe is with its own actions.

Before speaking more about the chances for "success" or "failure" of the reforms, it is useful to be clear about what success would mean. Many people say, "How can Eastern Europe succeed? The industry is so old-fashioned; the workers don't have the right skills; the enterprises are so dilapidated; the environment is despoiled." If "success" were to be defined as solving these problems and elevating Eastern European living standards to Western levels in a period of ten years, then Eastern Europe surely cannot succeed. By Western European standards, these countries will remain poor for a generation or more.

The term "success" should therefore mean something more modest, though certainly challenging enough. At a minimum, success should mean the consolidation of democratic institutions and a well-functioning market economy. As for a practical standard of future economic performance, I would suggest that reforms will have been successful if these countries pull close enough in living standards to Western Europe in the next decade or two that they can comfortably be integrated into the European Community. Poland, Hungary, and the Czech Republic are aiming for EC membership by the end of this decade, while the timetable might be somewhat longer for Romania or Bulgaria.

In the case of Poland, for example, an ambitious but achievable target would be that Poland have the same per capita income *relative* to the EC in the year 2000 that Portugal (the poorest EC country) had in 1986 when it became an EC member. This goal would require that Poland raise its living standards from about 37 percent of the EC average (Poland's position in 1989) to about 50 percent of the EC average (Portugal's position in 1985, on the eve of EC membership). Assuming that the EC grows at around 2.5 percent per year during the 1990s, this degree of convergence would require growth in Poland of around 6.4 percent per year during the years 1993–2000.[2] Such rapid and sustained growth would lead not only to a steady convergence in living standards with Western Europe, to a level that would justify Poland's accession in the EC, but would solidify the political base for economic reform and greatly legitimize the newly democratic institutions in the country.

It is also useful to have clearly in mind what a failure of the reforms might mean, because the concept of "failure" can also be misunderstood. At a minimum, failure could simply mean a continuation of economic stagnation or economic growth too slow to raise living standards toward those in Western Europe along the timetable just spelled out. But what worse could happen? Failure for Eastern Europe will not mean a reversion to communism. No matter how bad the economic situation, the countries of Eastern Europe will not return to the past system. Failure, rather, means the inability to reach any new consistent system, and particularly the Western European system, if I may call it that. The possibility of this kind of failure is very real because the political challenges of the Eastern European transformation are daunting, and indeed are far more complex than the economic challenges.

It is good to have a case study of utter failure, just as one has a model of success. If Spain is a role model for overcoming authoritarian rule and a backward autarkic economy, then Argentina between 1950 and 1989 provides an example of failure. Argentina is a country that went from having one of the highest living standards in the world sixty years ago to being a middle-income developing country today. What most characterized Argentina—and why it represents the kind of failure that might be seen in Eastern Europe—is that Argentina repeatedly failed to develop a political consensus in support of a market economy and economic integration with the outside world. Instead, over the last fifty years it has veered wildly between alternative sociopolitical models. The wild swings have led to repeated collapses of democracy, dangerous foreign policy adventures, internal violence, and of course, Argentina's dismal economic performance.

There are real risks in Eastern Europe that the political consensus in favor of reform will fail, because the extent of transformation will be so great. Nonetheless, even though Eastern Europe's economic tasks are greater than they have ever been in Argentina, the chances of success are also greater. The social consensus in Eastern Europe to rejoin Western Europe is stronger than any comparable consensus in Argentina on economic strategy during the past half century. If Eastern Europe's consensus can be sustained, the worst political nightmares in Eastern Europe can probably be avoided. If this consensus is not sustained (for a number of possible reasons, including Western European failure to respond adequately to the challenge ahead), the chance of chronic political instability, an absence of sustained economic policies, and vested interests blocking basic market reform—as have characterized Argentina—could be the economic future of Eastern Europe.

The political turmoil that will be engendered by Eastern Europe's social transformation will be huge, though in fact we should expect political turmoil with or without economic reform. There is simply no way to escape turmoil when one has gotten into a dead end and must make fundamental changes, and when a new set of basic norms (including a new constitution) must be established. Any meaningful strategy and set of tactics for reform must take into account the political minefield, not just as an aside but as the very centerpiece of thinking about change.

Poland's Struggle to Catch Up with Europe

Poland's radical reforms started with the fall of the communist regime in the summer of 1989, and the assumption of power of the Solidarity-led government of Prime Minister Tadeusz Mazowiecki. The new economics team, under the direction of Deputy Prime Minister Leszek Balcerowicz, prepared a comprehensive strategy of reform, which began to be implemented on January 1, 1990. To understand the strategy and tactics of reform, it is necessary to appreciate the economic situation that confronted the new government.

Minister Balcerowicz and his team confronted a legacy of communism that was adverse in almost all dimensions. The economy was both impoverished and deeply scarred in its basic structure by forty years of a nonmarket economy. The economy was also reeling from a profound financial crisis, building into hyperinflation, that resulted from the fundamental structural problems as well as the political and administrative collapse of the old regime.

Of course, the dominant characteristic of the Polish economy as of 1989 was that it lagged far behind the income and productivity levels of even the poorest countries of Western Europe. Therefore the great task facing Poland could most simply be described as the need to "catch up." Table 1.1 shows that Poland's GNP per capita lies between the averages for the lower-middle-income developing countries and the upper-middle-income developing countries, and far below the high-income industrialized countries (all according to World Bank classifications). Poland is far poorer than all of the countries of Western Europe, and is on a par with Argentina (it is not an accident that I used that analogy). It is also interesting, however, that in many social indicators Poland resembles Western Europe, despite being poor: life expectancy is higher than in comparable middle-income developing countries; infant mortality is considerably lower, though above that of the high-income countries; literacy is universal.[3]

Poland's relative impoverishment is reflected clearly in the low rate of ownership of consumer durables. Before the

Table 1.1
Social indicators of economic development

	Poland	LMI	UMI	HI
GNP per capita ($U.S.)	1,850	1,270	2,940	17,080
Health:				
Life expectancy (years, at birth)	71.4	63.8	67.2	76
Infant mortality (per 1,000 live births)	17.5	59.1	46.9	9.6
Education:				
Literacy (% of pop., 15+)	98.0	73.8	78.2	100.0
School enrollment (% of school-age pop.)				
Primary	101.0	106.8	103.5	101.9
Secondary	80.0	52.0	57.8	94.3
Tertiary	18	16	20	39
Consumer durables (no. per 1,000 persons):				
Telephones	12.5	6.3	11.1	50
Automobiles	10	3.7	7.1	33

Definitions: LMI, lower-middle income; UMI, upper-middle income; HI, high income.
Source: World Bank (1989) for all data except tertiary school enrollment, which comes from World Bank (1990).

start of reforms, durables ownership was at levels of the middle-income developing countries, though as we shall see, there has been a rapid increase in ownership of several types of durables since 1989. There were very few telephones (12 per 100 population in 1986–88), and these work poorly, leading Poles to quip that "half of Poland is waiting for a telephone, and the other half is waiting for a dial tone!" Notice how few automobiles there are, compared with Western Europe. In general, as one goes down the list of consumer durables, Poland was truly at the level of a middle-income developing country at the start of reforms, not even close to the level of the poor countries of Western Europe.

It is well to keep in mind that Poland and the rest of Eastern Europe have lagged behind Western Europe for centuries, though the gap existing today was surely aggravated by the disastrous years under communism. Historians have long debated the origins of Eastern Europe's relative backwardness (see Chirot, 1989, for a recent collection of essays on this issue). Among the main factors, historians point to the economic and political weakness of the cities of Eastern Europe in the fifteenth to nineteenth centuries; the consequent longer period of feudalism, including serfdom; and the strength of a benighted, autocratic nobility that blocked political liberalization, the spread of education to the peasantry, and the development of capitalistic property relations.

In the specific case of Poland, the weakness of reforms in the seventeenth and eighteenth centuries, and the chronic weakness of the Polish kings, who were subservient to the nobility, eventually led to the dismembering of the state in the late eighteenth century at the hands of the neighboring states: Prussia, Russia, and the Hapsburg Empire (see Davies, 1984). Early Polish industrialization began in the nineteenth century, mainly in the part of the country then in Prussia (around the iron ore deposits of Silesia) and in the part then in Russia (particularly the textile region around Lodz). The separate development under the three ruling empires meant that after Poland became a nation once again in 1918, its first few years of independence were taken up almost wholly with the task of state building, and of knitting together a unified monetary, fiscal, and legal system from the disparate elements inherited from the 125 years of partition. (For a readable account of Poland's twentieth-century history, see Korbonski, 1992.)

Even in the interwar period, Poland displayed a great resilience and capacity to overcome problems. But alas, a debilitating trade war with Weimar Germany, followed by the Great Depression, and then the disastrous Nazi invasion meant that the new state never had a chance to get off the ground economically. The devastation of World War II (the worst in all of Europe) was followed by Soviet domination and the communist period. Once again, Poland was denied the chance to become a normal part of Europe and to begin to catch up with Western nations that were far ahead in living standards.

Relative impoverishment was not the only legacy inherited from the communist period. There were several structural characteristics of the economy in 1989 that resulted directly from the long period of communist rule.[4] We will want to keep six structural features in mind as we discuss the reform strategy and the early results of the reforms. First, Poland (like the rest of Eastern Europe) is highly industrialized, because industrialization was the preeminent goal of the communist planners. In fact, Poland was *over*industrialized when compared with other countries at a comparable level of economic development, since the nonindustrial sectors, particularly services, were starved for resources as the converse of the industrialization drive. Second, Poland, almost alone in Europe, still has a large peasant agriculture sector. This large peasant sector, with low productivity and high political demands on the state, poses important problems of adjustment.

Third, the economy was overwhelmingly state owned, which is of course the key defining characteristic of socialism. Fourth, Poland lacked small- and medium-sized industrial enterprises, whether public or private, on the eve of reform. Fifth, Poland's international trade was excessively directed toward the East, as a result of the Soviet Union's postwar domination of Poland. Sixth, and perhaps the one favorable legacy, Poland was remarkably egalitarian in the distribution of income and wealth. In a word, almost everybody started the new era poor and without wealth.

A closer look at the data helps us to appreciate these points more deeply. Table 1.2 compares the structure of employment and output of Poland and the OECD countries. Several points are noteworthy. First, on the eve of market

Table 1.2
Distribution of employment and output by sector, Poland and OECD, 1988

	Poland	OECD
Distribution of labor force (percent)		
Agriculture	29.0	6.1
Industry	36.5	33.3
Mining	3.3	0.9
Manufacturing	25.4	24.3
Construction	7.8	8.1
Services	34.0	60.9
Transport and communications	7.5	5.8
Distribution	8.9	19.1
Finance	2.2	8.1
Other	15.4	27.9
Distribution of GDP (percent)		
Agriculture	13.0	2.8
Industry	60.7	33.0
Services	26.3	64.1

Source: *Economist* (1990), pp. 36 and 196.

reforms, Poland remained a highly agricultural economy, with agricultural employment standing at 29 percent, and with agricultural output at 13 percent of GNP. The employment share is a bit overstated, as many workers on the farm also worked part-time in industry, shops, or personal services. But even taking this into account, Poland still had a remarkably large though declining agricultural sector. Poland had so far not gone through the demographic shift from agriculture to nonagricultural employment that is characteristic of economic modernization. Most of Polish agriculture remains enormously unproductive—with traditional peasant farmers working on tiny, uneconomic plots that are too small to benefit from most modern technologies. Because a large proportion of the agricultural workforce is older farmers near retirement age, there is some evidence that the agricultural labor force is shrinking rapidly, especially under the pressures of market reform.

In addition to the high share of agriculture in employment and GNP, there is also a high share of industry. Indeed, the industrial share in total output, at 60.7 percent, is nearly *twice* the proportion of the OECD countries. Even allowing for some important measurement problems (an understatement of the size of the service sector, for reasons mentioned later), the overindustrialization of Poland, and the rest of Eastern Europe, is one of the most notable legacies of communism. The employment share in industry is also high, though not nearly as remarkable as the output share.

The counterpart of the large agricultural and industrial sectors was the incredibly small service sector at the start of the reforms—much smaller than that of Western Europe, especially if one excludes transport, which is sometimes put into the industry category. There was a relative dearth of employment in distribution services (wholesaling, retailing, catering, restauranting), finance, and even public administration. There were simply very few shops and restaurants, almost no bankers, and only a handful of private wholesalers to be found in a country of 40 million people. Shortages of basic services that we take for granted were the bane of daily life: the inability to call a plumber, the difficulty of having a car repaired, the need to wait hours simply to get at a personal bank account.[5] Moreover, many of the functions of distribution carried out by specialized wholesalers and retailers in a market system were carried out within industrial firms, and without the gains from specialization in service activities. As we shall see, this has all changed dramatically in just a couple of years. The service sector has been the boom sector in the Polish economy, creating well over a million new jobs and hundreds of thousands of enterprises in the first two years of reform.

Table 1.3 covers some of the same ground, but compares Poland with some of the poorer countries of Southern Europe, namely Greece, Portugal, and Spain. These are an important comparison group, as Poland differed little economically from these countries at the end of World War II. Moreover, these countries undertook, in the 1960s and 1970s, the kinds of policies that Poland must undertake today: opening the economy and adopting the institutions of Western Europe. As we see in the table, the share of employment in agriculture in Poland, Greece, Portugal, and Spain, was at about 40 percent as of 1960. By 1987, all of these countries have dropped to lower levels of agriculture than Poland, although Greece has had less of a transformation than the others (because of the poor economic policies in the 1980s). The Western European countries all experienced enormous growth in the service sector, which Poland did not. The transformation from 1960 to 1987 for the periphery of Europe entailed an enormous movement of the labor force out of agriculture and into services, and to a lesser extent into industry. In Poland, the labor that left

Table 1.3
Distribution of employment and output by sector, Poland and selected countries

Employment	1960			1975			1987		
	A	I	S	A	I	S	A	I	S
Poland	43	32	25	29	38	33	29	36	35
Greece	57	17	26	35	28	37	28	28	44
Portugal	44	31	25	34	34	32	23	34	43
Spain	38	30	31	22	38	40	16	33	51
GDP	1960			1975			1987		
	A	I	S	A	I	S	A	I	S
Poland	35	45	20	15	61	24	13	61	26
Greece	20	23	57	17	27	56	13	30	57
Portugal	24	34	42	14	39	47	9	40	51
Spain	21	34	46	9	37	54	5	37	58

Note: A = agriculture, I = industry, S = services.
Source: For Greece, Portugal, Spain, Finland, 1960 and 1975, OECD Main Economic Indicators; and 1987, *Economist* (1990). For Poland, 1960–87, national sources.

agriculture—and this was a smaller proportional drop than in the Western European countries—went into industry rather than services.

Table 1.4 makes the important if obvious point that Poland was largely state owned at the start of the reforms. But perhaps this table is useful nonetheless, for one major reason. I hope that no one will say after looking at this table, "Why privatize? There's plenty of state-owned industry in Western Europe!" This table shows that although there is state-owned industry in Western Europe, it comprises a small proportion of the economy compared to the proportion of industry owned by the state in Eastern Europe. State firms in the West operate in a market environment dominated by privately owned enterprises. And almost all Western European countries have been actively reducing the size

Table 1.4
Size of the state sector, measured by output and employment, various countries (percent)

Country	Output	Employment
Command economies		
Czechoslovakia (1986)	97.0	. . .
East Germany (1982)	96.5	94.2
Soviet Union (1985)	96.0	. . .
Poland (1985)	81.7	71.5
China (1984)	73.6	. . .
Hungary (1984)	65.2	69.9
Market economies[a]		
France (1982)	16.5	14.6
Austria (1978–79)	14.5	13.0
Italy (1982)	14.0	15.0
Turkey (1985)	11.2	20.0
Sweden	. . .	10.6
Finland	. . .	10.0
United Kingdom (1978)	11.1	8.2
West Germany (1982)	10.7	7.8
Portugal (1976)	9.7	. . .
Denmark (1974)	6.3	5.0
Greece (1979)	6.1	. . .
Norway	. . .	6.0
Spain (1979)	4.1	. . .
Netherlands (1971–73)	3.6	8.0
United States (1983)	1.3	1.8

a. Figures exclude government services, but include state-owned enterprises engaged in commercial activities.
Source: Lipton and Sachs (1990), drawing upon Milanovic (1989, tables 1.4 and 1.7).

of the state-enterprise sector throughout the 1980s, through programs of widespread privatization.

In Poland and the rest of Eastern Europe, state ownership of industry was almost 100 percent at the time of the 1989 revolution. In Poland, it is not a question of having a few dozen state-owned firms operating in the industrial sector, but of having 3,000 state-owned firms and very few private firms at the outset of reforms. The privatization problem is a totally different kind of problem from that of Western Europe, and it means that no matter what the ultimate model of ownership—whether Austria's mixed system or Mrs. Thatcher's vision of a completely private-ownership economy—Poland would have to move as radically and rapidly as possible toward privatization to have a Western ownership structure within this decade.

Table 1.5 points up another legacy of central planning. Central planners had no desire to coordinate the activities of hundreds or thousands of small firms in a sector if one large firm could do the job. A standard strategy, therefore, was to create one giant firm whenever possible. There was certainly no desire to allow for enough firms to engender market competition (which was not allowed in any event). What one finds in Poland is that the average number of workers per industrial enterprise at the start of reforms was quite large, much higher than in the West. In 1986, 58 percent of Poland's industrial workers in state-owned enterprises were employed in firms with more than 1,000 workers, whereas the comparable measure in a sample of Western economies was only 19 percent. On the eve of radical economic reforms, there were almost no small state industrial enterprises in Poland. In 1988 there were only 982 state enterprises with fewer than 100 employees. Poland completely lacked the standard market environment of many small and flexible industrial firms servicing the larger enterprises.

Other factors also contributed to industrial gigantism. Ideological imperatives were behind the trend toward giant firms, for Stalinist economists believed ardently in the benefits of economies of scale. An additional factor—which is very important to understand—is that in a shortage economy, no firm could rely on other firms to provide supplies on a steady basis. Therefore, firms strove to become autarkic units as much as possible, eschewing the division of labor

Table 1.5
Distribution of employment in industry by size of establishment, Poland, 1937 and 1986, and selected market economies

Country	Average number of workers per establishment	Percentage of workers in firms of size:			
		100 workers or fewer	101–500 workers	501–1,000 workers	More than 1,000 workers
Poland					
1937	54	33[a]	27	41[b]	n.a.
1986[c]	88	10	25	15	51[d]
State enterprises	378	6	21	16	58[e]
Cooperatives	30	42	54	4	1
Sample of Western economies[f]	30	35[g]	33	13	19
South Korea	n.a.	33[h]	67[i]		

n.a. Not available
a. Includes employees in establishments of between 6 and 100 employees.
b. Includes all employees in establishments with more than 501 employees.
c. Socialized sector. Employees in the private sector work in establishments with an average employment of 2 workers.
d. Seventeen percent of all workers are in establishments with employees greater than 5,000.
e. Nineteen percent of all workers are in establishments with employment greater than 5,000.
Austria, Belgium, France, Italy, Japan, and Sweden. Percentage of workers employed in total manufacturing excluding mining.
g. Includes employees in establishments of between 10 and 100 employees.
h. Includes employees in establishments of between 4 and 99 workers.
i. Includes all employees in establishments with employment greater than 100. Twelve percent of employees are in establishments with employment of 101–200; 11 percent are in establishments with employment of 201–300; and 44 percent are in establishments with employment greater than 300.
Source: Lipton and Sachs (1990).

in order to escape the vagaries of deliveries from other enterprises.

The situation was the opposite of Adam Smith's pin factory. A typical shoe manufacturer, for example, would not only manufacture shoes, but would make all of the necessary machine tools; would have its own metal working shop for machinery repairs; would do all of its own transport; would do all of its boxing; and would do its own packaging and labeling. A senior official in Poland gave me another example. At one point in the mid-1970s, when food supplies in the market became extremely unreliable, a major industrial enterprise asked this individual for advice on installing pigpens in the factory, so that the firm could raise pigs to provide food directly to the workers! This kind of autarky certainly undermines modern industrial efficiency.

Table 1.6 shows the structure of Poland's trade up to the beginning of the reforms: area I refers to the nonconvertible currency zone; area II refers to the convertible currency zone (the ordering is not incidental, but coincides with the traditional ordering of priorities). The share of exports and imports with the East, until 1989, was very high. The share dropped rapidly afterward, for reasons I will describe. More than half of the area I trade was with the Soviet Union.

Table 1.7, meanwhile, demonstrates another structural legacy of the communist period: a low degree of income inequality. Socialism succeeded in one goal: it made everybody equal, though equally poor. In the mid-1980s, Poland had an remarkably high share of income for the lowest quintile, 9.7 percent, and a very low share of income in the highest quintile, 35.2 percent. Under the communist system there were of course serious nonmarket distortions, in the form of disguised privileges, that increased income inequality above the levels shown by the official data. But even correcting for these would not alter the basic conclusion of an extremely narrow income distribution. The wealth distribution was also enormously equal—almost nobody had

Table 1.6
Structure of trade in the nonconvertible currency area (I) and convertible currency area (II)

Share of trade by trading area						
	1970	1980	1985	1988	1989	1990
Percent exports						
Area I	64.1	55.9	54.8	48.5	40.6	17.4[a]
Area II	35.9	44.1	45.2	51.5	59.4	82.6
Percent imports						
Area I	68.8	55.6	60.7	47.1	40.1	16.6[b]
Area II	31.2	44.4	39.3	52.9	59.9	83.4

a. Exports to the Soviet Union were 10.3 percent of the total.
b. Imports from the Soviet Union were 8.6 percent of the total.
Source: *Rocznik Statystyszny*, various issues.

Table 1.7
Income distribution in Poland and selected developing and developed countries

		Percentage share of household income (quintiles)				
	GNP per capita	Lowest	Second	Third	Fourth	Highest
Poland	1,860	9.7	14.2	18.0	22.9	35.2
Other middle-income countries						
Peru	1,300	1.9	5.1	11.0	21.0	61.0
Mexico	1,760	2.9	7.0	12.0	20.4	57.7
Brazil	2,160	2.4	5.7	10.7	18.6	62.6
Venezuela	3,250	4.7	9.2	14.0	21.5	50.6
Korea	3,600	5.7	11.2	15.4	22.4	45.3
High-income countries						
Spain	7,740	6.9	12.5	17.3	23.2	40.0
U.K.	12,810	5.8	11.5	18.2	25.0	39.5
Italy	13,330	6.8	12.0	16.7	23.5	41.0
Germany	18,480	6.8	12.7	17.8	24.1	38.7
U.S.	19,840	4.7	11.0	17.4	25.0	41.9
Japan	21,020	8.7	13.2	17.5	23.1	37.5

Sources: The income distribution data are from various years in the 1970s and 1980s, reported in the *World Bank Development Report* for 1989 and 1990, Table 30, for all countries except Peru, Mexico, and Korea, which are from the *World Bank Development Report, 1987*. GNP per capita from Table 1, *World Bank Development Report, 1990*.

any wealth, except in the case of private land or home ownership. The wealth was mostly in the hands of the government, in the form of state enterprises and state-owned apartments.

Poland is sure to experience an increase of income inequality as market reforms are introduced, but the key point is that Poland is highly equal at the start. Today's conditions are attractive—morally, ethically, and politically—for market-based reforms. We are not starting from a Brazilian or Peruvian situation, in which free-market reforms might be viewed with distress because of their likely effect of further widening an enormously uneven income distribution. In fact, it is fair to suppose that Poland started reforms from an *excessively* egalitarian society in the economic sense, in that income gaps between skilled and unskilled workers were too low to induce workers to invest adequately in human capital (through on-the-job training and formal education).

Poland and Spain Compared

Let me set the stage for the reforms by briefly comparing Poland and Spain (table 1.8). I believe that this is an interesting comparison because starting in 1950 these two countries had very similar economic conditions. They were both largely agricultural, Catholic, peripheral regions of Europe, that since the nineteenth century had lagged behind much of the rest of Europe in economic and political modernization. They arrived in the twentieth century with living standards among the lowest in Europe and with an unusually large proportion of the population still engaged in very inefficient smallholder agriculture. They both had disastrous experiences just before midcentury: Poland suffering the highest proportion of population loss in Europe during

Table 1.8
A comparison of Poland and Spain, 1950–1988

	Poland	Spain
Area (1,000 km^2)	313	505
Population (millions)		
1950	23.9	27.0
1988	37.9	39.0
Per capita income ($U.S.)		
1955[a]	755	516
1988	1,860	7,740
Industrial production		
1950[b]		
Cement	2,512	2,103
Pig iron	1,488	658
Steel ingots	2,515	818
1988[c]		
Crude steel	16.9	11.7
Cement	17.0	24.4
Electric energy	144	122
Industrial production per capita		
(U.K. 1900 = 100)		
1953	49	22
1963	88	43
1973	160	122
1980	196	156
Exports ($ billion)		
1950	0.6	0.4
1989	12.9[d]	43.3
Educational enrollment		
1965		
Primary	104	115
Secondary	69	38
Tertiary	18	6
1987		
Primary	101	113
Secondary	80	102
Tertiary	18	30

Table 1.8
(continued)

	Poland	Spain
Consumer durables (per 100, 1986–88)		
Automobiles	11.1	26.3
Televisions	22.7	35.7
Telephones	11.8	24.4
Radios	25.6	34.5

a. Reported in B. Balassa, "Growth Performance of Eastern European Economies and Comparable Western European Economies," *American Economic Review,* May 1970.
b. Cement, pig iron, steel ingots, in thousand tons.
c. Steel, million metric tons; cement, million tons; electricity, million kilowatt-hours.
d. Total exports are the sum of exports to the convertible currency area ($8.5 bl) and exports to the nonconvertible currency area ($4.3 bl). It is likely that the latter value overstates the market value of these exports if they were to be valued at world market prices.
Source: *Economist* (1990), World Bank (1990), national sources.

World War II, and Spain suffering its Civil War, which not only crushed democracy but stifled economic development.

The two countries had about the same population in 1950—about 25 million. They were also very close in per capita income terms. By one measure, Poland was slightly ahead in 1955, at $750 per capita as compared with $500 per capita in Spain, though the data are not very precise. Poland was also a larger industrial power than Spain in 1950. By 1988, however, Spain's per capita income was *four times* that of Poland's. This enormous jump in income was also reflected in Spain's greater ownership of consumer durables, and a much higher proportion of the population in tertiary education. Poland did retain its lead in a few industrial areas, such as steel and electricity production, but this is an illustration of Poland's incredible concentration of resources in heavy industry, rather than broad-based development.

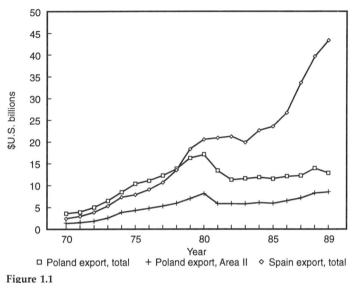

Figure 1.1
Exports of Poland and Spain, 1970–1989

The difference between the two countries—economic opening in Spain, continued isolation in Poland—shows up most dramatically in the differing export performance of the two countries, shown in figure 1.1. Until relatively recently, the export performance of the two countries was similar. Even as late as 1970, Poland's total dollar value of exports exceeded Spain's (though Poland's exports to area II, the convertible currency countries, were well below those of Spain). The dramatic shift came during the 1970s and 1980s, when Spain's export earnings surged ahead and Poland's stagnated.

So, starting from a similar point in the mid-1950s, Spain shot ahead of Poland in the next thirty-five years. Spain started to catch up with the rest of Western Europe, while Poland fell farther behind. The central reason for Spain's success was its shift from being economically isolated from the rest of Europe to being closely integrated with Europe. The shift started in the late 1950s, still under the Franco regime, when Spain began to reduce the trade and investment restrictions that had artificially isolated the Spanish economy. This shift toward integration with Europe accelerated greatly in the 1970s after the death of Generalissimo Franco. And finally, in the 1980s, Spain became a member of the European Community. Poland, by contrast, remained isolated from Western Europe, cut off by the Cold War, until the revolution of 1989. It did not reap the economic benefits that come with the opening, both political and economic, that Spain carried out.[6]

Close observers of the Spanish developments stress that the force behind Spain's reform, and the key to its economic success during the past decade, was the same as in Poland today: the desire to return to Europe after decades of isolation (see de la Dehesa, 1993). In 1959, the first impulses for trade liberalization came from a balance-of-payments crisis, and the consequent need to obtain international financial support as well as access to West European markets for new exports. Later on, after Franco's death, the powerful drive for harmonization with Europe helped the country to maintain an even keel in the first years of democratization.

Poland's Deepening Economic Crisis, 1970–1989

In the early 1970s, Poland's economic system was already showing signs of exhaustion. After worker protests in 1970, the new Gierek regime attempted to "jump-start" the economy by upgrading the technology of Polish industry, but without a change in the economic system. The main idea was to stimulate new exports by importing modern technology, while remaining squarely within the socialist economic framework. Between 1970 and 1977, Poland borrowed about $20 billion from Western governments and banks. The idea was simple, though wrong: that Poland did not need to change the economic system, but just to use better machinery. Remarkably, as with Argentina at around the same time, the huge amount of foreign borrowing produced almost no increase in Poland's exports to Western markets. As a result, the loans could not be repaid. Poland became one of the first countries in the world to fall into debt crisis after a round of heavy borrowing in the 1970s.

By the late 1970s, Poland's access to new loans had dried up, and Poland was struggling to make debt-service payments. The shift from capital inflows to capital outflows created a dramatic squeeze on the economy. Without access to new international loans, Poland's imports fell sharply. Polish enterprises found themselves cut off from imported raw materials and intermediate products that were needed to keep the factories going. And because part of the borrowing of the 1970s had been used to purchase consumer goods the cutoff in new loans also led directly to a reduction in the importation of consumer goods and increased shortages in the retail sector.

Under the weight of this cutback in imports, the economy plummeted after 1979, and living standards declined sharply. Yet despite the squeeze in domestic consumption and living standards, there was no rise in export capacity to Western Europe. Most of the debt service falling due simply went unpaid, and unpaid interest was simply added to Poland's bill. In this way, the debt grew from about $25 billion in 1978 to around $45 billion in 1991, with almost no new borrowing. The increase in debt was mostly the accumulation of unpaid interest over a period of more than a decade.

Thus the attempt to jump-start the old system by borrowing from abroad and building new factories produced almost no results, but instead led to a cataclysmic balance-of-payments crisis. It is a lesson that Gorbachev would have done well to ponder in the second half of the 1980s, when the Soviet Union went on a borrowing spree not unlike that of Poland in the 1970s. The result of course was the same: foreign borrowing could not substitute for fundamental economic reform.

The balance-of-payments crisis in Poland in 1979, and the related drop of national income, produced the outcry that led to the birth of Solidarity in 1980. Solidarity, of course, had great political successes in 1980 and 1981, but was crushed by martial law at the end of 1981. During the martial law period, there were a number of attempts at modest economic reforms, but they produced few real results. The economy stagnated until the end of the communist period.

I want to describe the failed economic reforms of the 1980s undertaken by the Polish communist regime, so that we can better comprehend what the Poles are trying to do today. What the Polish regime tried ran parallel to what Gorbachev attempted on the domestic side under *perestroika*—and it led to an almost identical economic debacle. Both Poland and the former Soviet Union ended the communist reform period with a hyperinflation, intense shortages in the state-run distribution system, a burgeoning black market, and sharply falling industrial production. The similarity of outcomes in both cases points to the deep flaws of the communist reform strategy. (Kornai [1986] provided a devastating portrait of the limitations of Hungary's communist reforms that foreshadows the failures of the *perestroika* reforms.)

What Gorbachev tried to do to some extent, and the Poles to a far greater extent, was to *decentralize* economic activity, but within the basic socialist framework. The main step was enterprise reform, promoted in both countries in the late 1980s, designed to give greater freedom to the state enterprises to set wages, inputs, and outputs (but, typically, not prices).

Two features of the reforms ultimately doomed them. First, the communist reformers never really believed in competition, so that decentralization did not lead to functioning markets. Prices remained controlled; entry by new firms into existing markets was discouraged; international trade remained restricted so that the international market provided no real competition for domestic producers; chronic shortages and excess demand meant that new enterprises could not get started or could not survive for the simple reason that they could not obtain necessary inputs. In short, existing state enterprises were never put to the market test, despite being given more freedom of maneuver. Second, the communist reformers had no interest in privatizing industry. They completely neglected or misjudged, or simply tolerated, the enormous inefficiencies that came from the lack of proper ownership of the enterprises. They failed to realize that the "insiders" of the enterprises, the management and workers, could seriously distort enterprise behavior to their own advantage. In essence, the communist reformers failed to understand the basic flaw of socialism, whether of a "market" variety or not: when there are no capitalists, there is nobody to represent the interests of capital.

Under the old "command economy," before the Gorbachev reforms, enterprise policies were controlled by central fiat, backed up by the threat of force against workers and managers who tried to evade the commands. When the commands, and the threat of force, were (mercifully) removed in the enterprise reforms in the second half of the 1980s, managers and workers attempted, not surprisingly, to increase their incomes at the expense of the state by absorbing whatever income flow and whatever assets they could from state enterprises. They demanded higher wages and stripped assets through various means—either overt or covert.

In any economy, of course, workers and managers would like to take home the profits or the assets of the firms, but usually shareholders are to some extent able to prevent that by instructing the manager to operate on their behalf. We know that corporate governance does not work perfectly—it seems to work less well in the Anglo-Saxon countries than some countries of continental Europe—but it works a great deal better than no corporate governance at all, which became the situation after the "corporate governance" once exercised by the communist party and the central planners was eliminated and enterprises were told to operate on their own.

The most obvious implication was that workers started to make demands for wage increases, which for many reasons managers did not resist. One reason is that in many cases the managers were actually selected by the workers themselves, or at least the workers' councils had a veto over the selection. Managers were scared of workers, and they remain scared of workers today—to an extent even greater now than before in many state-owned enterprises, because there are no counterbalances. In many enterprises, managers must run for annual election by workers' assemblies or workers' councils within the enterprise.

The result in Poland was the same as in Russia: as the terror of the Communist party was removed, a wage explosion ensued. In Poland this happened in 1980–81, during the rise of Solidarity, and it happened again in 1987–89. Figure 1.2 shows the rather stunning evolution of wages between 1985 and 1992 in both countries. The real wage is the index of wages divided by the index of prices. In both Poland and Russia, real wages shot up tremendously between 1987 and 1989, after the start of Gorbachev-style reforms.

If these were data from a market economy, you would say, "My word, what a great surge in living standards! Look

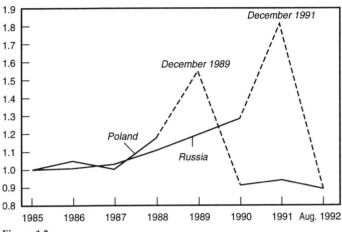

Figure 1.2
Real wage developments in Russia and Poland, 1985–1992 (wage index, 1985 = 1.0) Sources: Government of Russia and *Biuletyn Statystyczny* (monthly statistical bulletin), various issues. For Russia, the industrial real wage is shown. For Poland, the real wage for the six key sectors of the economy is shown. Wage data are annual averages, except for the year before the economic reform programs were introduced. For that year, the December real wage is shown by the dashed line to capture the peak. For Russia, the peak real wage was in December 1991. For Poland, the peak real wage was in December 1989. The last data point is the real wage for August 1992.

at how successful *perestroika* was—it has raised real wages in the Soviet Union by 70 percent between 1985 and 1991!" Of course, there was no productivity to back this increase in real wages, so that wage increases did not translate into more goods on the consumer market. The wage increases merely created *huge excess demand* and a massive intensification of *shortages*, rather than an increase in real purchasing power and in living standards. Since they resulted in longer queues with no increase in the overall supply of consumer goods, it is a good bet that the higher real wages actually led to a drop in living standards. In both Poland and the Soviet Union, the market socialism of the communist reformers proved to be a dead end.

After price liberalization, in Poland in 1990 and in Russia in 1992, the huge run-up in real wages was reversed, as is seen clearly in the figure. But as I shall stress again later, just as the increase in real wages during 1987–89 did not signify a rise in living standards, the reversal of the wage increase after price liberalization should not be interpreted as a sharp fall in living standards. To measure changes in living standards, different kinds of evidence must be used.

After the enterprises were granted autonomy in 1987, many other things happened that, like the wage increases, were designed to strip the enterprises of income and assets. One all-too-common form of activities falls under the rubric of "spontaneous privatization," or what in the West would be called stealing. Spontaneous privatization occurs when managers, or sometimes managers together with the workers' council or some other contingent of workers, gain ownership over state assets in one way or another. It did not take long for a state manager with no supervisory board of directors to realize that he could set up his own business, and then lease the entire factory to his new business (which might have one secretary in a little room) at a very low price, thereby taking all of the profits into his personal business, and leaving the state enterprise with huge losses, which he was able to cover with new loans from the state banks. Because of the government's fear of unemployment, it was willing to provide credits to loss-making firms.

Of course, many other ways have been found to milk state assets, for example in the context of joint ventures. In the absence of corporate governance, a joint venture may arise by a state manager telling a prospective foreign partner, "I will give you the enterprise for a very low price if you will give me a five-year contract, or a golden parachute, or 10 percent of the firm, [etc.]. I don't really own this, but I'm sure that we can get the deal through the bureaucracy."

In the last years of the communist regime, these kinds of abuses provoked a public outcry. This process of "spontaneous privatization" accelerated the revolution in Eastern Europe, because there was nothing more grating on the public than the notion that the communists who had ruined the economy over the past forty years were about to steal it and become the capitalist owners for the next forty years. In Poland in 1989, just before the fall of the old regime, public anger over this kind of behavior was intense.

The communist reformers failed in many other areas as well. Because they were hesitant to allow private-sector activity, they tended to accept that state enterprises must be kept alive at all costs, lest the plant shutdowns result in spiraling unemployment. They were unable to imagine or accept that new private firms would arise to absorb the workers who lost jobs in the existing enterprises. For this reason, they were also unenthusiastic about real competition for state enterprises; for tight credit policies that risked layoffs; and for subjecting the economy to international competition. Of course, since the state managers were the key to the political base of the communist regime in the last days, the managers themselves were able to do a great deal to make sure that reform measures were timid and would not place their enterprises in a real competitive environment.

In conclusion, market socialism has very deep and intrinsic flaws. Of course, the timidity of the reforms; the power of the *nomenklatura* to avoid a real opening of the economy to international competition, and even the introduction of domestic competition; the political illegitimacy of the regime; and the corruption and arrogance of the Communist party all contributed to the failure of the pre-1989 reforms.

Yet the problems went deeper. The communist reform period was doomed, because the system that Gorbachev, Jaruzelski, and others like them tried to implement was macroeconomically unstable and socially explosive. Socialism can work under a command system—if not efficiently, and not humanely, then at least with a certain coherence. It can do certain things such as building large factories and producing armaments, though it cannot provide a great deal of what the public wants. But ending the command system without working to establish competitive markets and private ownership as the basis of the new economy was a fatally flawed approach.

2   Poland's Big Bang

The partial economic reforms taken in the final years of the communist regime dismantled much of the central planning apparatus and allowed a small private sector to begin to develop. The reforms failed, however, because they were much too cautious in creating a real market environment, and because they were generally hostile to real privatization of the economy. The communist reformers paid too little attention to the distorted incentives facing the decentralized state enterprises, particularly with regard to excessive wage settlements. They were too timid to restrict credits to the enterprises, a policy that would have led to at least some restraint on wage inflation. And the communist reformers were of course locked in the old power structure, and so were uninterested in subjecting the state enterprises to real competition. They also tended either to participate in, or turn their eyes from, the socially noxious practices of "spontaneous privatization" discussed in the previous lecture.

The regime was, of course, also deeply illegitimate, and this represented a fundamental constraint on reforms. The government could not appeal to the public for restraint, patience, and trust—very important elements in any successful reform program. This political weakness was dramatically highlighted in 1987–88. With inflation, wages, and the budget deficit all rising sharply, the government tried to launch a macroeconomic stabilization program. The government in fact launched a referendum at the end of 1987, in which the people were asked to support a major stabilization program. The referendum failed. This was not surprising, in view of the deep public distrust of the regime, and in view of the fact that even in long-established democracies, the public is loath to vote for tax increases and price increases, even when this is "the right thing" to do.

Soon after the defeat of the referendum, the government announced that it would proceed anyway with the planned cuts in subsidies and increases in consumer prices, thereby confirming once again the public's mistrust. The cuts in subsidies were designed to reduce the budget deficit, but the whole episode developed into an enormous fiasco, repeated ironically by the Gorbachev regime three years later (although the capitalist world failed to follow Marxism's iron laws, it seems that the communist world followed fairly rigid "laws" of self-destruction). The result of the price increases, in combination with decentralized state enterprises and the weak political legitimacy of the government, was enormous labor unrest and a wage explosion. The attempt to reduce the real wage by eliminating consumer subsidies instead resulted in a sharp increase in the real wage. After the 15 percent increase between 1987 and 1988, real wages rose by another 9 percent on average between 1988 and 1989. As I have stressed, this increase in real wages was accompanied by growing hardships—queues, shortages, black markets—not higher living standards.

As the macroeconomic crisis deepened, the government saw the writing on the wall. With the political liberalization in the Soviet Union making possible a new political initiative inside Poland, President Jaruzelski called for a round-table discussion between the regime and the leading opposition forces, including key representatives of the banned Solidarity trade union. At the outset of the round-table discussions nobody foresaw that they would end not in political compromise, as the regime envisioned, but in the fall of the communist regime.

In the economic portion of the roundtable discussion, the Solidarity representatives acted to defend the interests of the workers in the context of a regime that was profoundly distrusted. It is not surprising, therefore, that Solidarity's major goal was to win an agreement on wage indexation as a transparent, automatic, and understandable means of pro-tecting living standards. Of course, as I shall stress, it was exactly the wrong recipe as part of an overall stabilization program, but in early 1989 nobody was yet thinking clearly about stabilization. As often happens in a political contest with a many competing groups, Solidarity soon found itself outflanked in its demands by the official communist trade union, which tried to establish its legitimacy with the work-ers by insisting on an even greater extent of indexation than Solidarity was advocating. When Solidarity economists said that the wage indexation coefficient should be 0.6 (meaning that the wage should be raised by 0.6 of 1 percent for each 1 percent increase in consumer prices), the communist trade union upped the ante by insisting on 100-percent wage indexation (meaning that the wage should be raised by 1 percent for each 1 percent increase in consumer prices). This was, in effect, a bidding war for the loyalties of the workers. The result of the economic talks was the introduction of a generous wage indexation scheme, with a coefficient of 0.8, a factor that soon proved to be an enormous problem, when real wages had to be reduced to sustainable levels by the Solidarity-led government that came to power just four months later.

Under the rountable agreement, elections were held in June 1989 for 35 percent of the lower house of the Polish parliament and 100 percent of the newly created upper

house, or senate. Solidarity, of course, won an overwhelming surprise victory. They lost one seat out of 100 in the
senate, to an independent candidate. Thirty-five communist
candidates for the lower house ran unopposed, but they still
had to get 50 percent of the votes cast. As it turned out, all
of the communist candidates but two actually lost because
most Poles carefully crossed out their names on the ballot.
Many Poles told me of the joy of bringing their children to
the polling station, and then having them participate in the
methodical striking of the detested names.

Solidarity itself was overwhelmed by the result. It is hard
to believe in retrospect, but Solidarity was not expecting
such a complete rout. However, new complexities immediately arose. The economy was collapsing and Solidarity
lacked any specific economic plans. In fact, up to the elections, Solidarity had not thought in any way, shape, or form
of actually taking the lead in forming a government. This
was, after all, still June of 1989, and the revolution of 1989
had not yet taken place. Poland was flanked to the West by
the Honecker regime in the GDR and to the South and East
by Ceausescu in Romania and Jakes in Czechoslovakia.
These regimes seemed solid to almost all observers (though
Adam Michnik, one of the most thoughtful political observers in the world, predicted to me in July 1989 the imminent collapse of the Jakes regime).

Almost no one imagined, though some of us hoped, that
within two months Solidarity would be fielding a team to
undertake a fundamental and massive restructuring of the
economy—an economic reform task more ambitious than
anything that had ever been attempted. Solidarity, as its
leaders kept stressing after the elections, was not even a
political party, much less one with a group of ministers
waiting in the wings. It was an anticommunist movement,
encompassing a large share of society, but one that did not
have the luxury, means, or need to formulate a clear pro-

gram. For this reason, Solidarity's economic strategy had to be designed with speed and urgency in the face of huge unknowns.

After the elections the old government resigned, and the communists tried to form a new government with parliamentary backing. In July, President Jaruzelski designated General Kiszczak to try to form a government. This was a peculiar choice to say the least: Kiszczak was a leader of the martial law crackdown of 1981, and had been personally responsible for the arrest and incarceration of many of the newly elected members of the parliament. As Kiszczak scrambled to put together a coalition, the outgoing government did something economically responsible but politically explosive. In response to gravely intensifying food shortages, it liberalized most food prices. This brave act resulted in another round of unrest, and quickly ended Kiszczak's attempts to form a new communist-led government.

Lech Walesa, in a typically brilliant maneuver, found unexpected coalition partners for Solidarity within the communist-dominated parliament—two small, nominally independent parties that had not been heard from for years, but which had started to look forward rather than backward and decided that their hopes lay with Solidarity. They therefore broke ranks with the communists and agreed to form a coalition government with Solidarity. With the communists retaining control over the state security apparatus, the new government took shape with Solidarity- designated ministers in the key economics posts. The Soviet Union (and Gorbachev personally) gave a green light to the proposed government.

With Solidarity on the verge of forming a government, the last general secretary of the communist party of Poland, Mieczyslaw Rakowski, made a last-ditch effort to hold on to power. The nature of his attempt was revealing.

Rakowski traveled around Poland to meetings of state managers, warning the directors that they would lose their
power in the event of a Solidarity government. When the
chips were down, the communist leaders turned to the
enterprise managers, their real base of support. But it was
too late. Communists and noncommunists alike in Poland
wanted something different, and even with the continued
opposition of many state managers, there was a broad consensus that Poland should escape from the past horrors and
move forward—and toward the West.

By this point the crisis had reached astounding propor-
tions. The inflation rate had reached 34 percent in the month
of August (an annual rate of more than 3,000 percent).
Wages were about to soar as the indexation clause of the
roundtable agreement kicked in. The budget deficit was
above 10 percent of GNP, all financed by central bank
money. The economy was careening toward hyperinflation,
defined as inflation of more than 50 percent per month. It
hit the hyperinflation threshold in October, when consumer
prices rose by 54 percent in the month (an annual rate of
more than 17,000 percent).

The term hyperinflation is sometimes casually tossed
about, even for inflation rates of a mere 100 or 200 percent
per year. The real beast, however, is both rare and potentially devastating to a society. Poland's hyperinflation in
1989 was just the fourteenth occurrence in world history. In
fact, Poland became only the second country to suffer two
bouts of the disease, in 1923–24 and 1989–90. The previous
repeat case was Poland's neighbor, Hungary, which had
hyperinflations in 1923–24 and 1945–46. Sadly, since Poland's outbreak of hyperinflation, there have been two
more: Yugoslavia and the former Soviet Union (FSU). The
FSU, in fact, is the third case of a repeater, since Russia
suffered hyperinflation after the revolution, and again in
1992.

Poland's hyperinflation, and the Russian hyperinflation that followed, had an important and peculiar characteristic. In a normal market economy, a monetary expansion produces a broad-based increase in prices. In Poland, however, price increases in most sectors were blocked by official controls on prices, administered by the ministry of finance. In these sectors, the monetary increase produced shortages and queues on the official markets, and an increased resort to black markets, on which prices soared. Thus the Polish hyperinflation was a mix of open inflation and repressed inflation, with soaring black-market prices and a growing resort to illegal trade and barter. (Weitzman [1991] provided a very insightful model of shortages and queuing in a situation of excess demand.)

In addition to skyrocketing inflation, money-financed budget deficits, and shortages, Poland suffered from a range of severe international finance problems. Most immediately, the balance of payments was collapsing as imports were running rapidly ahead of exports, draining reserves at the central bank. The black-market exchange rate was several times the official exchange rate, a phenomenon that imparted a profound anti-export bias to the economy (exporters received fewer zlotys per dollar of export earnings than they would have received in the free market for foreign exchange; thus the incentive for exports was diminished). Poland's foreign debt, at around $40 billion, was not being serviced. The country simply could not sustain the payments and so was in default to all of its international creditors.

The disastrous state of affairs prompted more of the black humor so famous in the region. I remember best a cartoon in a newspaper at the time Solidarity agreed to take power. It showed a plane crashing toward the earth, both engines aflame. We see President Jaruzelski walking toward the back of the plane with the steering column in his hand, leaning over to Lech Walesa, saying, "OK, now you try to fly this thing!" That captures the mood in the summer of 1989.

In July, the Solidarity leadership and parliamentary group engaged in an active analysis and debate over how to proceed. Key Solidarity leaders understood that their enormous political support should be translated into radical economic reforms. It is important to appreciate these political roots of Poland's economic reform strategy. Poland's strategy has been rightly perceived as very radical. It has been widely criticized as well as praised. But one of the criticisms—that this was a program designed by academics who did not understand politics, society, and so forth—is absolutely wrong. The notion of moving radically, rapidly, and decisively was strongly held by the political leadership of the Solidarity. It was in common understanding with the technocrats that Poland can and must make a clean break with the past. The Solidarity leadership recognized that such a radical course was necessary not only for economic success, but to consolidate postcommunist power. The "shock therapy" was not something applied as an intellectual construct by Polish technocrats or foreign advisors, and still less something imposed on Poland by the IMF, which was not even present at the formative stages of the program. The radical reforms resonated with the new democratic leaders, as well as with the economic needs of the society.

My colleague David Lipton and I had several long discussions in June and July with Poland's new political leaders to explain our views on a strategy for comprehensive economic reform. We stressed that the reforms could succeed, despite the enormity of the challenges that Solidarity would face. Many in the Solidarity leadership feared that Solidarity would simply be pawns of the communist old guard, because Solidarity lacked enough expertise to fill the ministries. They feared that Solidarity would be left to administer painful medicine but without the administrative personnel or policy instruments really necessary to guide the reforms, while communist bureaucrats could continue to frustrate the reforms.

It was here that economic logic and political logic coalesced. I stressed that the idea of radical reform was not just an economic strategy, but also a political strategy to overcome Solidarity's lack of personnel and control in the ministries (and indeed the lack of any qualified personnel at many key points in the administrative apparatus). The point was simple: if the reformers do not control the ministry of foreign economic relations, all the more reason to let the foreign exchange market allocate foreign exchange! If the reformers do not control the price division of the ministry of finance, all the more reason to let markets determine prices.

In the end, the Solidarity leadership took up the cause of radical reform, for several crucial reasons. They recognized that they had a unique opportunity to make an economic breakthrough to a market economy and a political breakthrough to democracy. They understood the economic and political logic of radical reforms. Their own experience had taught them that tinkering within the old system would produce no results. They knew that the economy bordered on hyperinflation. Economic logic also underscored the need to move comprehensively, as each aspect of the reform was intimately connected with the other dimensions. And Solidarity's lack of experienced personnel in the ministries also led the new government to rely on market forces as much as possible.

In mid-July, I was asked by the leadership to prepare an outline of such reforms.[1] The instructions from one of Solidarity's leaders were clear: "Give us the outline that you see fit. But make it a program of rapid and comprehensive change. And please, start the outline with the words, 'With this program, Poland will jump to the market economy.' We want to move quickly; that is the only way that this will make sense to our society, that it will make sense politically, and—as we understand from experts—the only way it will make sense economically as well."

The Balcerowicz Plan

On August 24, 1989, Tadeusz Mazowiecki became the first noncommunist prime minister of postwar Poland, with a Solidarity-led government in coalition with the former Communist party and its satellites. The Solidarity faction commanded the key economics ministries. The new prime minister understood the scale of the task ahead, as well as the opportunity to use Solidarity's enormous credibility to make a real breakthrough for Poland. I had the honor to meet with him on his first day of office, even before the economics team was selected. He knew what he wanted. In his words, he was "looking for his Ludwig Erhard" to carry out radical reforms on the scale of those carried out by postwar Germany. He found his man in Leszek Balcerowicz, a brilliant and bold economist who became the deputy prime minister for economy and the father of the "Balcerowicz Plan."

I met Balcerowicz soon after he had accepted the position of deputy prime minister, but before his public appointment. His first words were, "Yes, we will make a radical reform." Balcerowicz had been preparing for this opportunity for years, and had assembled a team of research economists around him who were prepared to help introduce and implement the reform measures. Balcerowicz held a vision of how Poland should proceed that was similar in concept to the program that Lipton and I had outlined for Solidarity in July. Balcerowicz invited us to work closely with his team, an opportunity that we eagerly accepted.

I want to describe in some detail the ideas of the Balcerowicz Plan, and the results of that plan during the first years. The key idea of course was to break decisively with the communist system, to end halfway reform, and as the Solidarity leaders had said, to jump to the market economy. The goal was to create an economy "in the style of Western Europe," based on private ownership, free markets, and integration into world markets. The plan also combined long-term market reform with a short-run emergency stabilization program to end the incipient hyperinflation. Balcerowicz understood extremely well from the experiences of Latin America that to break the back of a hyperinflation, half measures cannot work. The stabilization measures must be extraordinarily tough, because the disease is extraordinarily virulent. If it is not ended, it tends to run out of the control of policymakers.

Balcerowicz and his team saw that almost none of the countries in Latin America had been successful in ending a hyperinflation. While Poland was confronting its hyperinflation, there were simultaneous hyperinflations in Nicaragua, Peru, Argentina, Brazil, and Yugoslavia—an extraordinary array of experiences with which to make comparisons. They noted that up to that point there had been only one successful end to a hyperinflation in the 1980s, the case of Bolivia, a country that had moved most dramatically and rapidly against the hyperinflation. President Raúl Alfonsín of Argentina, President Alan Garcia of Peru, and President José Sarnay of Brazil had shared the mistaken notion that a gradual tightening of monetary and fiscal policy would provide a more tranquil and socially stabilizing way to end hyperinflation, but the results of gradualism were decisively negative in all of those countries.

The main pillars of the reform were clear. The first was macroeconomic stabilization. The second can be put under the very broad rubric of liberalization—the range of actions needed to allow markets to function. Liberalization includes the end of central planning; the end of bureaucratic controls over prices, international trade, and the use of raw materials; and the establishment of a legal environment to support decentralized actions of private property owners, including a commercial code, company law, and system of judicial enforcement of contracts. The third pillar was privatization—the transfer of ownership of state assets to the private sector. The fourth was the construction of a "social safety net" adequate for the new market economy that would take shape. Most urgently there was the need to introduce an unemployment compensation system. The fifth pillar of the Balcerowicz Plan was to mobilize international financial assistance to support the transformation.

As for the most urgent task, macroeconomic stabilization, there was enormous international experience, including both success stories—Bolivia, Israel, Mexico—and failures throughout Latin America. The success stories all pointed to a single main conclusion. The stabilization program should involve a package of monetary and fiscal measures designed to cut decisively the rate of credit expansion from the National Bank of Poland to the government and to the enterprises. By tightening the expansion of domestic credit, it would be possible to stabilize the market exchange rate as well as domestic prices.

At a general level, liberalization was also relatively well understood. Part of it is simple—get the planners out of the process. The state planning commission was actually turned into an analysis and forecasting unit—a transformation that worked well, though problems remained as bureaucrats tried to reassert their power. The price-setting unit in the ministry of finance was simply disbanded. Other aspects of liberalization were also easier to effect than might appear at first glance. The legal structure was not as bad as one might assume, because the previous communist regime had actually undertaken a number of steps to resurrect Poland's legal codes of the interwar period. There was a 1934 commercial code; there were lawyers who could negotiate and enforce contracts; there was a judicial system, which was rusty to be sure, but which was assigned the task of enforcing private arrangements. That part of liberalization therefore did not represent an impossible task.

The greatest conceptual breakthrough in liberalization was the rapid introduction of free trade. The importance of rapid trade liberalization in the Polish reforms cannot be overstated. By opening up the economy to trade, Poland's reformers aimed to accomplish several things. In the long term, of course, they sought to improve the efficiency of the economy through increased specialization. But in the short term, they aimed to use international trade to help establish competition for their domestic industries. Even with domestic industries heavily monopolized, open trade would help Poland to "import" a realistic set of prices for industrial goods, after decades in which prices had been set by the bureaucracy. In view of the importance and novelty of the quick move to free trade, I will return to this theme in detail later in this lecture.

The fourth and fifth pillars of reform, creating a social safety net and mobilizing international financial assistance, are also areas of significant and relevant international experience. The most urgent social policy concern was the establishment of a system of unemployment benefits, which did not exist under the old regime. In addition there was the need to switch from across-the-board subsidies (such as for foodstuffs) to targeted relief for vulnerable groups in the population. In other areas of social policy, the problem was a long-term redesign of pension, education, job training, and health-care systems. As for international assistance, special issues arose concerning balance-of-payments support, debt relief, and targeted emergency assistance at the start of the reforms, but as with the other areas, a broad framework for cooperation existed through international institutions and the European Community. As I shall describe later, the aid has been crucial, though sometimes it has come too slowly and grudgingly.

It is in the area of privatization that the reform government was faced with its greatest intellectual and political challenges. International experience in privatization often proved more misleading than helpful. It did no good for Poland to seek to emulate the United Kingdom, for example, in the design of a privatization program. Although the United Kingdom privatized about 50 enterprises in the course of a decade, Poland had more than 7,000 state-owned enterprises, most of which needed to be put in private hands. The sheer logistical effort, in addition to the profound political complexity of transferring the bulk of productive capital to private owners in a short period of time, demanded new arrangements.

In the remainder of this lecture, I will focus on the first two tasks, stabilization and liberalization. In the next lecture, I will turn my attention to the remaining three areas.

The Big Bang

Poland's stabilization and liberalization program was introduced dramatically on January 1, 1990, and it soon became known as "the big bang." The program was based on a few straightforward ideas. First, to eliminate shortages and allow markets to function, virtually all prices were decontrolled on January 1, 1990. Second, to cut the budget deficit and eliminate hyperinflationary pressures, most subsidies to households (especially food subsidies) and industry were slashed or eliminated entirely at the same date. Overall budget spending was restrained, through sharp cuts in public investment and subsidies. Monetary policy was also tightened substantially. Cheap credits to industry were discontinued, and the central bank rediscount rate (on loans to commercial banks) was raised sharply, even brutally, at the start of the reforms. The central bank established credit targets to hold overall money growth to levels consistent with a rapid elimination of inflation. To establish a free-trade regime, the currency was sharply devalued and made convertible from the start, and the zloty-dollar exchange rate was maintained at the stable rate of 9,500 zlotys per dollar throughout 1990. Existing restrictions on international trade were almost entirely lifted. Trade licenses and quotas were generally abandoned (with a few exceptions) and tariffs were kept low.

The most dramatic move was the across-the-board elimination of price controls, which was designed to release the pent-up inflationary pressures that had emerged from past increases of wages and the money supply, and enormous budget deficits that Poland was running. It was expected that the overall price level would jump sharply at the start of the reforms. Subsequently, the inflation was expected to subside quickly, as long as the new monetary and fiscal policies were appropriate. In other words, the plan aimed for a *one-time* jump in the price level, to be followed by low inflation.

The idea of linking price liberalization and trade liberalization helped the reformers to cut the Gordian knot that had stymied their thinking for years. Polish industry was dominated by giant firms that were oligopolistic or monopolistic in their sectors. Reformers throughout the 1980s asked themselves, "How can we free up prices in this monopolistic setting? If we do so, all we will get is an explosion of monopoly prices and monopoly profits, which will be extraordinarily damaging politically as well as economically. On the other hand, how can we restructure these enterprises or subject them to competition in the absence of market-based prices?" Clearly, demonopolization would take a considerable amount of time: new firms would have to enter, and old monopolistic units would have to be sub-divided where possible, a process that is time consuming and often technically and politically difficult.

The rapid opening of international trade provided a simple and effective breakthrough to the problem. Although Polish industry is monopolistic within the confines of the small domestic market, it is hardly monopolistic within the confines of the European market. If the economy could be decisively opened up, there would be no need to worry about industrial monopoly, because the giant firms in Poland are small players in the European market. International competition would provide the competition in the internal market that Polish firms themselves would not provide at the start. If free trade could be introduced, prices could be liberalized.

For free trade to be introduced, two kinds of steps were needed. The first was an elimination of artificial trade barriers of various sorts, including licenses for permission to trade, various other kinds of approvals for specific commodities, an end of restrictive quotas on imports and exports, and low tariff barriers. The second half of the free-trade mechanism was financial: making the Polish currency convertible for trade purposes, so that domestic enterprises with zlotys could convert them to dollars for purposes of making imports.

Unfortunately, the issue of convertibility was clouded in myth and misunderstanding. Basically, convertibility was understood to be something so good that it could only be aimed for, like the holy grail, but never achieved, or at least not in a short time! Without understanding the economics at hand, many Polish economists and international economists remembered one thing: European nations had required more than a decade after the end of World War II to reestablish currency convertibility. The World Bank gave the Polish government in 1989 a document calling for a five-year transition to partial convertibility. The idea of immediate convertibility seemed out of the question to most observers.

Many economists and businesspeople, both within and outside Poland, argued that the zloty could not be convertible because Poland was too uncompetitive and had very low productivity. But this is tantamount to saying that the country is too poor and unproductive to engage in free international trade. This is, of course, nonsense. Ricardo taught us that trade depends on *comparative* advantage, not absolute advantage. Any country can engage in free trade, and similarly, any country can have a convertible currency.

Let's start with some definitions. In essence, convertibility means that there is a market for foreign exchange in which buyers and sellers transact at a unified market price. For example, when a Polish exporter sells his dollars in the market in return for zlotys, he receives the same number of zlotys that the buyer pays for each dollar of foreign exchange (aside from a small commission). Inconvertibility arises when exporters and importers face different prices, because of rules that limit their direct participation in the foreign exchange market. This was the case in prereform Poland and the rest of the CMEA countries. In the late 1980s, exporters had to sell part or all of their foreign exchange earnings to the central bank at an "official commercial" rate that was far below the free market rate (e.g., 1,000 zlotys per dollar at a time when the market rate was 4,000 zlotys per dollar). Importers were divided into categories. Some got foreign exchange from the central bank at the low rate; others paid the market rate; and still others were prohibited from participating in the foreign exchange market altogether.[2]

Convertibility can be achieved with the stroke of a pen simply by discontinuing the state's role in the foreign exchange market. Buyers of foreign exchange (importers) and sellers (exporters) are allowed to transact without restriction; artificial rates other than the market rate are discontinued. Favored importers are no longer benefitted by access to foreign exchange at preferential rates. Thus, by ending the nonmarket rates set by the central bank, convertibility can be achieved immediately. Of course, immediate convertibility causes disruptions in old arrangements, though of a favorable sort overall. Exporters immediately face improved export incentives, since they do not have to sell their dollars at an artificially low price (in terms of the zloty). Previously priviliged importers lose out, for now they have to pay the full market rate for foreign exchange. For importers that were previously paying the market rate, the change may be small at the start. Over time, however, as export earnings increase, the exchange rate tends to strengthen (at least in inflation-adjusted terms), so that the domestic cost of foreign exchange goes down. Imports became cheaper. (For the theory of currency convertibility, with an empirical analysis of the case of Poland, see Berg and Sachs, 1992.)

What is harder to achieve immediately is convertibility together with *exchange rate stability*. Convertibility just means a unified market price for foreign exchange, but not necessarily a stable price for foreign exchange. If monetary and fiscal policies are inflationary, the price of foreign exchange will continue to rise (along with other prices in the economy). As excessive zloty credits are issued by the central bank, those credits will be used in part to try to purchase foreign exchange, thereby driving up the price of the dollar in terms of the zloty.

The key therefore to a stable market exchange rate is keep a tight rein on monetary policy. With tight monetary policy and a floating exchange rate, the market price of foreign exchange will remain stable. The government might decide to carry this one step further, by announcing a *pegged* exchange rate. In that case, the central bank commits to buying and selling foreign exchange at a stated, stable rate. It can do this only if the chosen rate is close to what the floating exchange rate would be, and if monetary policy is maintained in such a way that the floating rate would also be stable. At the start of the big bang, Poland set its exchange rate at 9,500 zlotys per dollar, which was slightly *more* depreciated than the black-market rate at the end of 1989. The overdevaluation compared to the black-market rate caused a bit more inflation at the start of the program than would have occurred with a more appreciated exchange rate, but in return, the newly set exchange rate was easier to defend.

If the central bank issues so many zloty credits that the floating rate would depreciate, the counterpart under a pegged exchange rate is a loss of foreign exchange reserves. Households and firms take their excess zlotys to the foreign exchange market for conversion into dollars, and the central bank has to sell its own foreign reserves to meet the market demand. Eventually, it would run out of foreign exchange reserves, and the pegged rate would collapse.

In the case of Poland, the central bank started with a very low level of foreign exchange reserves. For this reason, monetary policy had to be especially tight. In fact, it was not enough merely to prevent a further decline in reserves. It was advisable to make monetary conditions so tight that households and enterprises would have to convert some of the foreign money that they had salted away—under the mattress or in foreign bank accounts—back into zlotys in order to carry out their domestic transactions. This is in fact what happened in Poland. There was a remarkable turn-around in the foreign exchange market at the start of the stabilization program. The flight from zlotys turned into a flight into zlotys; households actually queued at the exchange houses in order to turn their dollar savings into zlotys in order to build up sufficient real money balances.[3] In effect, the central bank sold zlotys and bought up dollars, thereby increasing the meagre foreign exchange reserves.

One additional factor made stability an achievable goal at the start: the creation by the leading industrial nations of a $1 billion stabilization fund to help back the zloty. The stabilization fund was a mix of grants and credits totaling $1 billion that the central bank could draw on to defend the zloty in the event that the bank was required to sell dollars to maintain the rate. The fund worked like deposit insurance: its mere presence meant that it was less likely to be used, because it helped to avert a panicked "run" on the zloty. Since households and enterprises knew that the exchange rate could be pegged at least for a while, they were less likely to convert their zlotys into dollars at the start of the program, when convertibility was introduced. After the zloty maintained its value for a while, confidence in the currency rose further. In the end, the stabilization fund never had to be drawn on to support the currency.[4]

To summarize, the logic of quick convertibility went along the following lines. The basic goal was to move from a situation of extreme shortages and hyperinflation to one of supply-and-demand balance and stable prices. For this Poland needed tight macroeconomic policies with the decontrol of prices. To have a working price system, Poland needed competition. To have competition, it needed free international trade to counteract the monopolistic industrial structure. To have free trade, it needed not only low tariffs but the convertibility of currency. To have convertibility of currency at a stable exchange rate, it needed monetary discipline and a realistic exchange rate.

Much of this is familiar classical economic medicine, but of course major doubts were raised about its application to Poland. Could it work in a socialist economy? The Polish reformers had no doubt that the stabilization and liberalization would work better if the firms were already privately owned. But even with state-owned industry, the reformers rightly believed that they could get started successfully if care were taken to plug the worst leak of the decentralized socialist economy: the lack of wage discipline. We noted earlier that the enterprises used their increased autonomy after 1987 to raise wages because there were no owners in the firm with an interest in the firm's profitability. Now, as part of the stabilization program, the government tried to exercise at least one ownership function—restraining wage increases—by putting temporary wage controls in place.

The specific form of the controls was a tax on wage increases above a statistically determined norm, partially indexed on inflation. The excess wage tax, known as the "popiwek," naturally became the focal point of tremendous political pressures on the government. The popiwek was crude medicine, but it was a necessary concomittant to macroeconomic policy under conditions of almost universal state ownership of industry. The popiwek offered enough control over wages in the short term to get the stabilization program started, but there could also be no illusions. Centralized incomes policies like the popiwek are economically inefficient and politically unpopular, and have a rapid obsolescence in the political marketplace. The popiwek would have to be replaced sooner rather than later by market-based wage setting built around true private ownership of enterprises.

The economic inefficiency of the popiwek was increased by an added political element. Because the government did not want to be seen to "punish" state-sector workers compared with private-sector workers, the popiwek was initially applied to both state and private-sector firms even though the logic of the policy was based on the absence of private ownership in large state-owned industry. This extension of incomes policy to private firms was doubly harmful: it limited the ability of the private sector to grow, and it weakened the government's fundamental claim to be building private property rights. For these reasons, after one year and at some political cost, the popiwek was completely removed from private-sector firms.

Price decontrol combined with trade liberalization, macroeconomic stabilization, and the popiwek did the job it set out to do. It allowed Poland to end the hyperinflation; eliminate shortages; create a convertible currency; "import" a set of international prices into the domestic industrial sector; and provide the basis for the rapid development of the private sector. As we shall describe, the state industries also responded to the new incentives, at least partially. They cut costs and increased exports significantly. Certainly the response would have been better with private firms, but there was an important response nonetheless.

Critics of this economic approach have often asked, "Why not privatize first?" If the real problem is lack of ownership rights, why not undertake privatization quickly, before taking these other measures? The answer is very simple. In the artificial world of an economics textbook, privatization should surely come first (in fact, in the textbook world, industry wouldn't be nationalized in the first place!). In the real world, however, Poland was facing imminent hyperinflation and a collapse of the economy. There was the inevitability (however frustrating) of an extended public debate about the strategy of privatization. And the logistical measures needed to privatize several thousand enterprises would require years in any case. It was simply not possible, therefore, to make substantial progress on privatization before addressing the pressing needs of stabilization and liberalization. The government and its mandate would have been swept away well before the public has finished its debate over the various approaches to privatization!

Let me underscore as well that it was as important to spur the new private sector as it was to privatize the existing state sector. The "big bang" policies made it possible for the private sector to grow rapidly during 1990 and 1991, even before extensive privatization of industry had begun. Any significant delay in stabilizing and liberalizing, in the belief that privatization should come first, would have had a highly deleterious effect on the spontaneous growth of the new private sector.

Living with Shock Therapy

After three hectic months of preparation, including rounding up some necessary international support—an IMF loan and a stabilization fund—the Polish big bang started on January 1, 1990. The key steps were implemented as planned: a sharp cut in consumer and producer subsidies; an end to almost all price controls; an elimination of central planning; a devaluation of the zloty-dollar exchange rate, followed by a pegged rate at the new level; an opening of foreign trade, including a suspension of licensing and quotas, and full convertibility of the currency for current account transactions; the introduction of the popiwek; and the introduction of various legal changes designed to encourage new entry of private firms, competition, and demonopolization. Privatization of industry was to have started early in 1990, but it was not until June that the framework privatization law was passed. Even before the passage of the law, however, small shops began to be privatized by local governments through auctions and leases.

What were the results of this program? We can best evaluate the results by reference to the major goals of the program: ending hyperinflation and shortages, making the transition to a market economy, and encouraging a structural change from heavy industry to light industry and services. In every area, there was substantial progress, though problems remain even three years after the start of the reforms. The progress has in fact been greater than generally understood, as the official data tend to give a systematically biased account, understating the benefits of change and overstating the costs.

The dramatic changes started on the first days of the program, with an enormous jolt to the economy that was quickly christened "shock therapy." With the elimination of price controls, the inflationary pressure that had been building up for years was suddenly released. The average price level jumped by about 80 percent in the first two weeks of January. It was a gut-wrenching experience for the public and the reformers alike. I was very confident that price explosion would soon end, but it was frightening to watch nonetheless. Would panic set in, with the government reestablishing price controls? Would a rock be thrown through a bakery window, thereby setting off social unrest? Would farmers continue to hoard their foodstuffs in expectation of even higher prices, or would food start to flow to the marketplace?

The results of the first few days were unimpressive to say the least. The farmers hoarded the grain and meat in expectation of still higher prices. Many economic pundits in the country commented in the press how horribly wrong the neoclassical Western economists were—they just did not understand anything about Poland. In Poland, the pundits asserted, when prices go up, shortages intensify. The program was attacked as "shock without therapy." Well, thank goodness, the farmers' speculation did not last long. After a couple of weeks, the food prices peaked, and some even started to fall. At that point, a flood of foodstuffs came onto the market as farmers realized that they were going to be left with enormous inventories with falling prices. By the third week in January, the major cities in Poland were inundated with thousands of farmers bringing food directly to the market—bypassing the state distribution system, setting up shop out of the trunks of cars, putting down blankets bearing meat, chicken, vegetables, or fruit. The real therapy had begun!

As a result of post–World War II protocols, Poles were able to enter West Berlin without visas, and large numbers of trucks and cars started to make the short trek between Warsaw and Berlin to load up on consumer appliances, fruit, and clothing in short supply in Poland. Suddenly, it was possible to buy fresh fruit on the street corners of Warsaw in the middle of winter for the first time since 1939. Poles marveled at the stocks of bananas, kiwis, and strawberries. It was heartening to hear older shoppers murmur, "Just like before the war." I spent a lot of time loitering among the new food stalls at that time watching the spontaneous organization of the consumer market.

The response of the old guard was interesting. As soon as the farmers started to come to the market, the minister of internal trade, a member of one of the small parties previously aligned with the communists, started to protest. He argued that the street trade should be licensed and kept on a small, regulated scale. This was yet another illustration as to why communist-led reform does not work. Had it not been for Balcerowicz as head of the economic team saying, "You will not touch those people—they're the reason we're doing this," the incipient private sector probably would have been suppressed. In the end, the street trade was not suppressed, and as the old restraints were removed, new private activity flourished. The blankets on which the food was placed in January became table stands by March, covered awnings by May, wooden sheds by July, and electrified, refrigerated kiosks by November.

By the third week of January, the price explosion had ended. Some prices actually started to fall. A few state-owned outlets started to advertise special sales on consumer appliances such as washing machines that had been in short supply for years. Nonetheless the public had sticker shock after a rapid doubling of prices. Anxieties were very high. It took a combination of moral suasion in the form of an appeal for Polish democracy, the excess wage tax (popiwek), and very tight credit policies to prevent enterprises from raising wages in line with prices. In the end, the wages did not respond.

The success of price stabilization is shown in table 2.1. We see that after the 77 percent rise in January 1990, price increases were 16 percent during the next month, and just 4.5 percent after that. In the two-and-a-half years of stabilization following the big bang, price inflation continued at a rate generally between 0 and 4 percent per month, on a gradual downward trend. The zloty-dollar exchange rate remained stable during the first sixteen months of the reform, until May 1991, when it was devalued by 14 percent. There was no drain of foreign exchange reserves as the result of the move to convertibility. In fact, there was actually an accumulation of foreign exchange reserves of about $2.2 billion for 1990. The dollar value of the wage rose sharply, from about $35 per month (at the free-market exchange rate) in June 1989, to $100 per month in January 1990, to around $200 per month in June 1992.

The stabilization program had achieved a pivotal success, but a view spread that the costs to living standards had been very high. With price increases outstripping wages in January 1990, the idea spread that the Balcerowicz Plan had substantially cut real incomes. Comparing November 1989 and January 1990, it appeared that real wages had fallen by around 30 percent. It was widely reported throughout Poland and the world that the big bang had started a remarkable process of change and an end of shortages, but at a fearful cost of falling living standards, "down by around

Table 2.1
Macroeconomic indicators, 1989–1992

	Real wage (1985 = 100)	Inflation (monthly rate)	Unemployment rate	Industrial production (1989 = 100)
1989: 1	102	9.6		110
2	121	8.8		99
3	148	8.1		110
4	130	9.2		101
5	118	6.8	0.0	104
6	128	6.1		109
7	125	10.3		86
8	179	39.5		92
9	135	34.2		99
10	109	54.8		101
11	116	22.4		94
12	142	18.3		96
Average	129	19.0	0.0	100
1990: 1	82	77.3	0.3	78
2	82	15.8	0.9	69
3	107	4.5	1.5	76
4	92	6.7	2.0	70
5	84	4.5	2.5	74
6	81	3.8	3.2	74
7	85	4.9	3.9	70
8	87	1.8	4.6	75
9	89	4.6	5.2	75
10	95	5.7	5.7	83
11	108	4.9	6.1	79
12	101	5.9	6.3	73
Average	91	11.7	3.5	75
1991: 1	87	17.2	6.8	72
2	91	6.7	7.0	64
3	89	4.5	7.3	69
4	85	2.6	7.5	63
5	79	2.7	7.9	61
6	76	4.9	8.6	62
7	81	0.1	9.6	59
8	79	0.7	10.1	59
9	78	4.3	10.7	60
10	81	3.2	11.1	65
11	88	3.2	11.4	59
12	90	3.1	11.8	59
Average	84	4.4	9.2	63

Table 2.1
(continued)

	Real wage (1985 = 100)	Inflation (monthly rate)	Unemployment rate	Industrial production (1989 = 100)
1992: 1	79	7.5	12.1	61
2	77	1.8	12.4	58
3	83	2.0	12.1	69
4	81	3.7	12.2	65
5	73	4.0	12.3	63
6	73	1.6	12.6	67
7	78	1.4	13.1	65
8	75	2.7	13.4	63
9	75	5.3	13.6	68
10	77	3.0	13.5	71
11	85	2.3	13.5	na
Average	78	3.2	12.8	65

Source: Inflation, real wage, and industrial production from the IMF *International Financial Statistics*. Unemployment from the *Biuletyn Statystyczny*, various issues.

one third." This alleged drop in living standards was largely illusory, since back in November 1989 Poles faced crippling shortages at the official prices, so that living standards on the eve of reform were much lower than the official statistics had suggested.[5] We will return to the question of price liberalization and living standards during 1989 through 1991.

Hundreds of thousands of new private businesses opened up in the wake of the reforms, as shown in table 2.2. Now it was possible to operate a private business: you could register the business; actually get the parts you needed without having to bribe a dozen bureaucrats; and if you had any supply shortages, you could just hop across to Helsinki or Berlin or to any other nearby Western market to import the needed inputs. Land and storefronts were sold or leased by local governments. Factories also sold machinery and inventories to individuals and new small businesses

Table 2.2
Private business establishments, 1989–1992 (number, in 000s, at year end)

	Commercial law partnerships	Joint ventures	Individual proprietorships
1989	11.6	0.4	813.5
1990	29.6	1.6	1,135.5
1991	45.1	4.8	1,420.0
1992 (mid-year)	51.2	7.6	1,523.4

Source: *Biuletyn Statystyczny,* various issues. Commercial law partnerships refer to private companies registered under the Commercial Code, including partnerships, limited liability companies, and joint-stock companies. Individual proprietorships are termed "individual business establishments" in the Polish data.

in order to raise enough revenues to pay wages and repay debts. (For a more detailed analysis of the remarkable dynamism of Poland's small private businesses, see Johnson, 1992).

The number of registered small businesses rose by 710,000 from the end of 1989 to mid-1992, as we see in table 2.2. This increase in small business owners represents around 4 percent of the working population! Total employment in these small businesses rose from 1,475,500 to 2,800,400, an increase of more than 7 percent of the total labor force. As for larger enterprises, the number of private commercial law partnerships (partnerships, limited liability companies, and joint-stock companies) rose from 11,693 at the end of 1989 to 51,174 by mid-1992. No one knows the true count of small businesses, as there is probably enormous tax evasion among very small firms, and a significant gray-market economy.

With the right to export at a realistic market exchange rate, and with the new ease of importing materials needed for producing export goods, Poland's enterprises, both state and private, achieved a veritable boom in exports to Western markets, shown in table 2.3. Exports to the convertible currency area rose from $7.6 billion in 1989 to $10.9 billion in 1990–quite a remarkable increase in a single year. In 1991, the export drive continued, with exports rising to $12.8 billion, and in 1992 exports were projected to exceed $14 billion. Poland was able to enjoy an import boom paid for by surging exports, with imports from the convertible currency area rising from $7.3 billion in 1989 to a projected $13.7 billion in 1992.

It is worthwhile noting that the export boom came as a surprise to most observers (except those aware of the export booms that had followed previous episodes of trade liberalization in other parts of the world, such as in China and Turkey at the end of the 1970s and beginning of the 1980s). After two decades of failed export promotion, most Polish analysts ascribed the failure to generate growing exports as a reflection of the low quality of Polish goods rather than of the profound anti-export bias of the old system (due to an overvalued exchange rate, excess domestic demand, and explicit trade barriers). Importantly, the export boom was broadly diversified and included many sectors, such as consumer appliances, in which almost nobody thought that Poland would have a chance of staking out an international market.[6] Poland's experience highlights again the futility of trying to guess the areas of a country's trade competitive-

Table 2.3
Poland's merchandise exports and imports in convertible currencies, 1980–91 ($ billion)

	1980	1985	1989	1990	1991
Exports	7.4	5.1	7.6	10.9	12.8
Imports	8.2	4.0	7.3	8.6	12.7
Balance	−0.2	1.1	0.2	2.2	0.1

Source: United Nations Economic Commission for Europe, *Economic Bulletin for Europe*, Vol. 44, 1992, Appendix Table 10, p. 138.

ness, and still less the possibility of picking the sectors for export growth. Inevitably, successful trade penetration must be based on the activities of individual enterprises in a hospitable macroeconomic environment.

The newly liberalized trade system disciplined the state sector remarkably effectively. One could watch the effects of new international competition on Polish firms already in March or April 1990, even before the state enterprises knew exactly what had hit them. If you wanted to print a book, you could now get paper in Helsinki. You did not have to beg the state-owned paper firm for supplies. State managers would report, "My God, our customers [other state enterprises] are telling us we have to cut our prices or they will shift their purchases to Finnish suppliers. What are we supposed to do? We're going to be terribly squeezed. We will have to force our own suppliers to cut their costs." One saw this chain of discipline growing over time—not instantly in January, and certainly not as powerfully in March or April as in October or November 1990, but state firms suddenly found that there were alternative suppliers, that there was real competition for the first time in decades. State enterprises started to learn to adjust their prices to match the competition from abroad.

The underpinning of the macroeconomic stabilization was the increased budgetary discipline, combined with an end of cheap credits to industry. The budgetary swing was enormous. As shown in table 2.4, the budget went from a deficit of 7.1 percent of GDP in 1989 to a surplus of 2.7 percent of GDP in 1990, a shift of nearly 10 percentage points. Two major items accounted for the sharp swing. First, subsidies were cut from 12.5 percent of GDP to 7.1 percent of GDP, as budgetary subsidies on food and industrial production were cut sharply (major subsidies remained on coal, transport, and household rents and utilities, which

Table 2.4
Poland: Budget summary, 1987–91 (percent of GDP)

	1987	1988	1989	1990	1991[a]
Total revenue	34.3	35.6	29.7	32.5	22.8
Turnover tax	10.6	10.9	8.8	6.5	6.6
Income tax	11.5	12.9	9.7	14.0	5.8
Other	12.1	11.9	11.2	12.0	10.4
Total expenditure	37.8	37.0	35.7	31.9	27.3
Wages, goods, services	12.9	12.4	13.4	15.3	12.2
Subsidies	15.4	16.0	12.5	7.1	3.7
Transfers to social funds	1.5	1.5	2.3	2.7	4.7
Investment	5.6	5.3	4.1	3.6	1.9
Other	2.5	1.8	3.3	3.2	4.7
State budget balance	−3.5	−1.4	−5.9	0.6	−4.5
Extrabudgetary funds balance	2.7	1.4	−1.2	2.1	−0.5
Local government balance	—	—	—	—	0.5
General government					
Revenue	48.2	49.0	41.8	44.6	37.4
Expenditures	49.0	49.1	48.9	41.9	41.8
Balance	−0.8	0.0	−7.1	2.7	−4.4
Financing	0.8	0.0	7.1	−2.7	4.4
Change in arrears	0.0	0.0	1.9	−0.3	0.9
Domestic banks	0.0	0.0	5.0	−2.6	4.4
Other domestic financing	0.0	0.0	0.5	0.1	0.0
Foreign financing	0.0	0.0	−0.3	−0.7	−0.1
Other	0.8	0.0	0.0	0.7	−0.9

a. Local government operations were excluded from the state budget for the first time in 1991. In 1991, local government revenues and expenditures amounted to 3.5 of GDP.
Source: de Crombrugghe and Lipton (1992), Table A.1 based on the 1991 *Statistical Yearbook of Poland* and the Ministry of Finance of Poland.

were scaled back further in 1991 and 1992). Second, the income (profits) tax on enterprises increased sharply, after price liberalization and wage controls restored enterprise profit margins. Of the two changes, only the subsidy cuts would be sustained in 1991. Enterprise income taxes plummetted in 1991, as enterprise profits fell sharply for several reasons, including rising energy prices to enterprises and a loss of export markets in the Soviet Union.

Living Standards, Unemployment, and Production after the Big Bang

That there was considerable good news after the big bang—an end of shortages, new businesses, an export boom—was quite apparent to visitors to Poland and to the Poles themselves, but what about the costs of the stabilization program? Attempts to make such programs costless to everyone tend actually make them disastrously costly to all. Many countries in Latin America have simply plunged back into hyperinflation after a brief period of stabilization when the government has felt that the economy should be "boosted up" to avoid hardships or unemployment. The soft heart in this case is also the soft head. We should expect some costs to some groups, but the question is, how large have they been? Was there a way to significantly reduce them without risk to the very process of stabilization and liberalization?

The usual listing of the costs is well known, because it is almost a mantra repeated by reporters and political opponents of the reforms: living standards down by a third, unemployment soaring, and real output down by 30 percent. All of that sounds rather dreadful, but fortunately it reflects an exaggeration of the costs of transformation, rather than real disaster. There has been no significant fall in living standards. Real incomes did not plummet. Unemployment, while high, is not soaring to the levels that were feared. And the lost production reflects the cutbacks in production of enterprises that lack customers, mainly the cutback of Poland's excessively large heavy industrial sector.

Figure 1.2 showed the real wage developments in Poland during 1985–92. The real wage index is the nominal wage of the industrial worker—the average monthly zloty income—divided by the cost-of-living index. We already noted in the first lecture that the real wage rose sharply between 1987 and 1989, and then fell sharply upon the big bang. Of course, none of that wage increase after 1987 reflected an increase in worker productivity. Instead, it reflected an explosion of worker unrest in the waning days of communism, as well as the natural effects of granting autonomy to state enterprises that lacked real owners to bargain with the workers.

Between December 1989 and January 1990, there was a precipitous fall from an index of 140 down to about 80, (with 1985 = 100), a fall of 42 percent. For 1990 as a whole, the real wage was about 30 percent below the real wage in 1989, but only 9 percent below the level in 1987. Therefore, the widely reported decline of "one-third" in real wages was based on a comparison with the excessive real wage level of 1989, a level that had helped to produce extreme shortages in the consumer market and incipient hyperinflation. Nonetheless, in journalistic and political discussions of the real wage decline after 1989, there was almost no mention of the fact that 1989 itself was an unsustainably high baseline. (Even the 1987 real wage level was an inappropriate standard for comparison with 1990, since there were shortages and queues in 1987 as well, though not nearly as severe as in 1989.)

In an economy plagued by shortages, it is silly to use the swing in the real wage as a measure of changes in living standards. Already in 1987, workers could not readily turn their pay into consumer goods. When the real wage rose from 1987 to 1989, workers were not better off, since the shortages intensified. Workers found that they were waiting in line for more hours, or forced to transact more in the black market, where prices were soaring to two or more times above the official prices. In other words, the prices used in the consumer price index did not really measure the cost of purchases, because the official prices did not reflect the shortages, queues, and black market prices caused by the excess demand on the consumer market. Similarly, when the real wage fell from 1989 to 1990, the result was not a comparable loss in real consumption, since the real wage decline was accompanied by a vast increase in the quality, quantity, and variety of goods available, as well as a disappearance of the queues and black markets.

For these reasons, the right way to measure the change in living standards is not by the change in real wage, but rather by the change in actual real consumption. What did people consume before and after the price liberalization? Was there a dramatic cutback in food consumption, such as a shift from meat consumption to starches? Did households cut back on their other purchases, of clothing, consumer durables, and so forth? This is the real evidence to assess. Fortunately, there is some information about consumption patterns from household expenditure surveys that have been conducted in Poland for many years. This evidence strongly refutes the idea of a calamitous decline in living standards as the result of price liberalization.

Evidence on food consumption is shown in table 2.5. As we can see, Poles on average consumed *more* meats and fruits in 1991 than in 1989, despite the alleged drop in real purchasing power. Contrary to popular conceptions, this was true of pensioners' as well as employees' households. There was a small decline in meat consumption for farmer and farm-employee households (constituting around one fourth of all households), but from much higher levels than city workers. Fruit consumption went up for all groups except farmer households. In any event, there is absolutely no evidence of any sharp drop in real consumption of meats and fruits after price liberalization.

The data on changes in Polish ownership of consumer durables render even more silly the vision of Poland in

Table 2.5
Meat and fruit consumption, 1989 and 1991 (average monthly kg per capita)

Type of household	1989	1991	Percent change
		Meat	
Employees	5.01	5.11	2.0
Employee farmers	5.45	5.32	–2.3
Farmers	6.66	6.47	–2.9
Retired persons and pensioners	5.70	6.34	11.2
Average (weighted)	5.42	5.56	2.6
		Fruits	
Employees	3.00	3.35	11.7
Employee farmers	2.72	2.86	5.1
Farmers	3.16	3.01	–4.7
Retired persons and pensioners	3.81	4.20	10.2
Average (weighted)	3.14	3.41	8.6

Source: *Biuletyn Statystyczny*, various issues, Table 46, "Average monthly per capita consumption of selected foodstuffs of households." The weighted average uses weights from 1991 data, and are as follows: employees' households, 52 percent; worker farmers' households, 15.2 percent; farmers' households, 12 percent; pensioners' and retired persons' households, 20.8 percent.

depression. As seen in table 2.6, the proportion of households owning major consumer durables showed a significant increase between 1988 and 1991 for virtually every category of durable. The Poles were starved for consumer goods for forty years. Now, with free trade, currency convertibility, and the rapid expansion of the retail sector, there is a ready availability of these goods, and Poles have been expanding their ownership of consumer durables rapidly.

Berg and I (1992) looked at a more comprehensive group of consumer items, including food, clothing, and consumer durables, to assess the changes between 1989 and 1990.

Table 2.6
End-of-year stocks of consumer durables per 100 households (workers' households)

	1988	1991
Radio	88.9	91.1
of which stereo	22.6	38.9
Portable radio	68.7	58.6
Color TV	41.7	82.9
Video player	1.9	41.0
Tape recorder	68.8	81.5
of which stereo	20.6	46.0
Bicycle	93.2	93.3
Car	30.2	38.3
Automatic washing machine	55.5	67.2
Refrigerator	100.0	99.9
Freezer	16.4	27.4
Vacuum cleaner	96.2	97.6
Sewing machine	60.7	59.6
of which electric	43.7	47.0

Source: Główny Urzad Statystyczny (Central Statistical Office), *Survey of Workers' Households*, 1992.

Using consumer expenditure data, we found that the weighted volume of consumption fell in 1990 compared with 1989 by around 4 percent, *not taking into account the rise in product variety, product quality, or the end of queuing time.* Starting from our estimates on real consumption flows, Roberts (1992) computed the additional gains from the time saved in queuing, and found that "the welfare gains from price liberalization were very significant" (p. 21).

If we take into account the additional gains in real consumption between 1990 and 1991, which even official statistics put at around 2 percent, we can safely conclude that, counter to the superficial judgments based on the statistical real wages, average living standards in Poland were higher in 1991 than in 1989.[7] Even if there is error in these estimates, and real living standards are lower on average in 1991 than in 1989, there are absolutely *no* grounds for believing that there has been a sharp fall of living standards as the result of rapid reforms.

Nor do the Poles themselves believe it. A survey in November 1991 asked Poles to assess their living conditions almost two years after the start of the reforms (see Ammeter-Inquirer, 1992). Their responses demonstrate a positive response on balance to the economic changes. Fully 82 percent of the respondents held that their family's economic situation was the same or better than five years before.[8] This was at a time in which the popular press depicted the Poles as seething with unhappiness over the hardships of the reforms. Similarly, 43 percent of respondents preferred "an economy like we now have," to "a socialist economy like before the revolution," while 24 percent preferred the socialist economy, and 33 percent saw no difference.

One undoubted cost of reform is the rise in unemployment, shown in table 2.1. Journalistic accounts of unemployment have often been alarming: unemployment in Poland climbs to 60,000; unemployment in Poland swells to 120,000; unemployment in Poland breeches the 1 million barrier; and so on. It is true that unemployment has risen significantly, but it is rarely stated that even with a million unemployed in 1990, the unemployment rate in Poland happened to be the same as in the United States and the United Kingdom—about 6.5 percent. By 1991, the unemployment rate had risen to about 13 percent of the labor force, quite high by Western European standards. But here too there were strong reasons for believing that the data exaggerated the situation. The unemployment rates in the major cities remained very low, around 5 percent, with the exception of Lodz, the old textile center, where unemployment was more than 15 percent. The unemployment was highest in the rural areas, and Polish analysts have concluded that a significant number of those reporting unemployment are in fact working in the second economy, or on the farms, and are collecting unemployment compensation as a form of income supplement for their other jobs.

It is widely estimated, within the Polish government and by independent experts, that around one-third of the unemployed fall within this category. The actual unemployment rate is probably closer to two-thirds of the measured rate, perhaps 9 percent of the labor force. Notably, among the unemployed, only about 23 percent as of December 1991 had lost their jobs as a result of so-called collective dismissal, in which companies lay off groups of workers. There are many voluntary job leavers among the unemployed and many new entrants to the work force (particularly school leavers), as well as the third or so of the unemployed that actually have jobs.

The main implication is that the shocking forecasts made by some critics at the start of reforms—that 30 percent of the Polish labor force would be unemployed, that the state sector would go bankrupt—have proven to be wrong. Unemployment did rise significantly, but to levels of Western Europe. The main reason that the dire forecasts proved wrong is that perhaps two million jobs have been created in new firms, especially in the new service sector. Hundreds of thousands of people who were no longer needed in the steel mills are working in shops, in distribution, and in retailing—a significant gain in the country's well-being. Although the official statistics hide much of what is happening, they clearly show that the transformation has not resulted in mass unemployment.

One can usefully distinguish Poland's experience from that of East Germany, where unemployment is much greater. On official measure, the unemployment rate reached 18 percent of the labor force at the end of 1992, but the actual rate is higher, because many workers that are now "part time" are in fact working almost no hours at all. The fundamental difference in the two countries is that in East Germany, wages shot up to levels far above productivity, as a result of political promises made by West German politicians and pressures for East German wage increases emanating from West German trade unions afraid of being undercut by low-wage production. In East Germany wages quickly went to around 50–60 percent of the West German level, whereas in Poland the wages remained at about 10 percent of the West German level—not lower than they were before, but also not much higher. Because East German productivity is around 30 percent of West German productivity, while wages are more than 50 percent of West German levels, virtually all of the state enterprises in East Germany are losing money right now. In Poland, on the other hand, most of the state enterprises are making money or breaking even at the much lower wage levels.

People often ask what the unemployment rate is going to be in the future. There will be more layoffs, but the unemployment rate will depend a great deal on whether Poland's wage restraint continues to hold. If wages start to rise ahead of productivity improvements, as they have in East Germany, or in Spain in the late 1970s, then there could be much higher unemployment. If the wage restraint remains a firm fact of political and economic life, the transformation can be carried forward with the same or falling unemployment. So the choice is really grounded in the politics and economics of wage setting.

Finally, let us turn to the widely discussed decline in industrial output, which fell by around one fourth in 1990 compared with 1989, and by more than 10 percent in 1991. In 1992, the industrial production began to rise, by 3.5 percent. Some critics charge that Poland's industrial decline is itself tantamount to a depression. Such criticism neglects the basic point that economies emerging from Stalinism have too much industry *compared with other sectors of the economy.* Therefore, when market-based economic transformation begins, industrial production declines while nonindustrial production expands, particularly in trade, finance, and services. This is a desirable transformation, not a deep recession or depression.

Polish economists and journalists have focussed their attention on industrial production for two reasons. One reason is that industry was the *idée fixe* of socialism for forty years, the basic standard for judging economic development. The sorry state of the service sector as of 1989 was the proof of this fixation. The second reason is related: the statistical agencies did not report data on key parts of the nonindustrial economy; economists and policymakers were not used to looking at the monthly index of retail sales, or housing starts, as in a a market economy. In fact, in the traditional socialist national accounts, production of services was not even counted (the focus was on net *material product*).

The sizable decline in industrial production is surely not a simple result of "shock therapy." *All* of the countries in Eastern Europe have experienced a sharp decline in industrial production, whether they have reformed rapidly, slowly, or not at all. In fact, comparing the large countries of the region, we see in table 2.7 that Poland has had the smallest cumulative decline in industrial production since 1989, and that it was the only country to turn around from decline to growth in 1992. As in Poland, the service sectors throughout the rest of Eastern Europe have been the main beneficiaries of the decline in industrial production, as workers and resources freed from the overgrown industrial sector have migrated to shops, wholesaling, finance, and other service areas.

Even if we restrict our attention to industry, there are some important points to note. Polish industry has gone through three phases. Industrial production fell sharply

Table 2.7
Industrial production in Eastern Europe, 1989–92

	1990	1991	1992	Cumulative change 1989–1992
Poland	−24.2	−11.9	3.5	−30.1
Bulgaria	−12.6	−23.3	−15.0	−43.0
Czechoslovakia	−3.5	−21.2	−10.6	−32.0
Hungary	−4.5	−19.1	−9.8	−30.3
Romania	−19.0	−22.7	−22.0	−51.2

Source: 1990–91 from United Nations Economic Commission for Europe, *Economic Bulletin for Europe*, Vol. 44, 1992, Table 1.3.1, p. 26. 1992 from national sources.

during 1990 with the beginning of the reforms. It fell further in 1991, largely as the result of the collapse of Poland's traditional exports to the Soviet market. (This is why Finland, which was closely linked to the former Soviet Union via trade, also suffered a sharp drop in industrial production in 1991.) By early 1992, however, a recovery was under way, compared with the very depressed levels of 1991. By September 1992 production was about 14 percent above the levels of a year before. As shown in table 2.8, which shows real sales of various industrial sectors, the industries that have sustained the largest declines in sales since December 1990 tend to be those that were closely linked to the Soviet market, and particularly the military-industrial complex: engineering, transport equipment, and precision instruments. The sectors that have grown the most since the end of 1990 are building materials, wood products (including furniture), pottery, apparel, and food processing. Note also that the drop in measured industrial production after 1989 probably overstates the real fall, because the official index almost surely undercounts the contribution to production of new, small-scale, private industrial enterprises.

The data on living standards, unemployment, and production reveal a society in transformation. Although overall

Table 2.8
Industrial sales (December 1989 = 100)

Sector	Dec. 90	Sept. 91	Sept. 92	Sept. 92/ Dec. 90
Coal	70	66	65	.93
Fuel	69	54	66	.96
Power	91	87	61	.67
Iron and steel	97	68	79	.81
Nonferrous metals	69	55	57	.83
Metal products	73	51	63	.86
Engineering	67	49	51	.76
Precision instruments	67	29	35	.52
Transport equipment	69	29	42	.61
Electronics	77	52	62	.81
Chemicals	74	56	67	.91
Building materials	88	88	105	1.19
Glass products	70	63	68	.97
Pottery	56	53	62	1.10
Wood products	78	70	92	1.18
Paper products	99	90	93	.94
Textiles	63	55	60	.95
Apparel	70	57	72	1.03
Leather	65	55	62	.95
Food processing	91	83	92	1.01
Total industry	76	59	67	.88

Source: *Biuletyn Statystyczny*, various issues.

consumption levels have not plummeted, there have surely been losers as well as winners in the transformation process. Though careful research has not yet elucidated the patterns of gains and losses on a detailed microeconomic level, we can at least make some educated guesses about the distribution of benefits. Among major social groups that have probably suffered a setback in living standards, we can cite peasant farmers, who lost large budgetary subsidies, and industrial workers in traditional heavy industry. High rural unemployment, political protests by peasant groups, and evidence of declining farm consumption (as we saw in table 2.5) suggest the losses to small farmers. It is also likely that older workers have fared worse than younger workers, because of the lesser mobility of the older workers, and that unskilled workers have fared worse than skilled workers, because the old system artificially compressed wage differentials between skill levels. Contrary to some journalistic accounts, the real consumption of pensioners seems to have been relatively well protected.

The basic conclusions on the results of the big bang are clear. Poland is in the midst of a profound transformation, which is creating private ownership (now producing more than 50 percent of GDP); a market system; an export boom (with convertible currency exports up from $8 billion in 1988 to around $14 billion in 1992); an end to the misery of shortages and queuing; a shift from heavy industry to consumer industry and services; and a chance for a normal economic life integrated in Western Europe, with realistic prospects of converging living standards in the future. Economic life remains hard in Poland. It always has been, and had been getting worse fast at the end of the 1980s. But it did not get still worse after 1989. The population has lived with great uncertainties after the start of radical economic reforms, but these are now diminishing. The economic future looks brighter.

3   The Return to Europe

In the first two lectures I discussed the five pillars of an economic transition to a market economy: stabilization, liberalization, privatization, creation of a social safety net, and economic support from the West. We have examined in some detail the results of Poland's big bang. We noted as well the great successes and the painful dislocations—especially higher unemployment—and the inevitable decline in the old heavy industries. After three years, however, the reform agenda is still incomplete, as the last three pillars of the reform are not yet fully in place. In this lecture, I would like turn to these issues. In addition, I will speculate on several related matters, including Poland's growth prospects; the differences and similarities with the other countries of Eastern Europe; and briefly on a question of overwhelming significance, the prospects of Russia's economic reforms.

Privatization in Poland

I have repeatedly stressed the pathologies that result from the absence of a proper ownership structure in Eastern Europe and the former Soviet Union. The experience of reform communism throughout the region has proved that the concept of market socialism—that is, a market economy with state-owned rather than private enteprises—should be laid to rest as a viable concept, much less a desirable one. It is an arrangement that invites irresponsible behavior by workers and managers, who are left free to strip the income and the assets of their enterprises. Wage pressures are relentless. Only real owners have the incentive to provide real governance over the use of the enterprises' assets.

In the Polish context, rapid privatization of large industrial enterprises has become ever more urgent now that a basic degree of stabilization and liberalization has been achieved. There is a race against time in taking the final step of transforming the state's property into private property. If this step is too long delayed, Poland's macroeconomic successes to date could still be reversed. The incessant financial pressures from the state-enterprise sector could still thrust Poland (and much of the rest of Eastern Europe) back into a situation of sustained macroeconomic instability. As we know from the experiences of Latin America, renewed macroeconomic instability could translate into political instability.

In Poland the risk of a renewed inflationary explosion is felt daily by the monetary and fiscal authorities of the state. As a stopgap measure, wages in the state enterprises are being controlled by an incomes policy, in the form of an excess wage tax (the popiwek). Incomes policies may work for a short time, especially when there is a widespread consensus (as was the case in Poland in 1990) that major groups in the country should exercise self-control to help the country overcome an acute crisis. But all incomes policies sooner or later become lightning rods of political opposition, especially as the urgency of a stabilization crisis begins to diminish.

The lack of enterprise self-discipline in wage setting is illustrated by the enterprises' response to the popiwek itself. Under the law, an enterprise that exceeds the wage norm must pay the government 5 zlotys for each 1 zloty of wage payments above the norm. It is hard to imagine a private firm willingly incurring a 500 percent tax on a wage increase; shareholders would be livid at such a trade-off. Nonetheless, by the end of 1990 more than 1,000 Polish state enterprises were voluntarily subjecting themselves to the popiwek by paying wages above the norm! In the socialist firm, after all, workers might as well maximize take-home pay, even at the cost of punitive taxes on the enterprise's earnings. They have little interest in having the firm retain its earnings, and still less in having the firm transfer its profits to the state. Ironically, the pressure for wage increases is often strongest in loss-making enterprises. If the firm is going under anyway, the workers are interested in grabbing whatever income they can before they are forced to find alternative employment. Thus, the enterprises even sell off machinery and use the proceeds to pay wages.

A second and related reason to privatize quickly is that the state enterprises will not properly manage the decisions over long-term investments. In a private firm, the owners will chose to make a long-term capital investment if it increases the present discounted value of future cash flow, even if the increased cash flow will not result for many years. In Poland's state-owned firms, however, there are no clear owners to reap the benefits of long-term investment. Workers and managers do not know whether they will be at the firm when a long-term investment comes to fruition, and they do not know whether their future wages and salaries would necessarily increase as a result. In general, the best bet of the current insiders is to maximize their own current income, come what may.

At this point, a skeptic might ask, "But what about China? Hasn't China maintained state ownership and yet succeeded in growing rapidly?" The answer is yes, but the Chinese policymakers themselves know that state ownership has been a hindrance, not a help, to their economic growth since the start of reforms. It is estimated that two-thirds or more of all state-owned enterprises are losing money in China.[1] This has been a chronic and serious threat to macroeconomic stability. Moreover, the great dynamism of the country has come in the nonstate sector, including township and village enterprises and joint ventures. For this reason, Chinese policymakers have begun to acknowledge the need for widespread corporatization and privatization.

If privatization proceeds too slowly, there is the risk that managers and workers within the enterprise might paralyze the privatization process at some point in the future. As time goes on, the managers and workers may come to view the enterprise simply as their own, because they face no real outside control and because they alone exercise many of the property rights of the firm. These insiders are therefore increasingly prone to protest any form of privatization that does not substantially benefit themselves. Alternatively, the insiders might simply find ways to privatize "spontaneously," by appropriating the assets in hidden ways.

If explicit privatization is too long delayed, the pressures will rise to give the enterprises directly to the workers and managers. This "solution," however, would have serious ethical and efficiency shortcomings. Workers in state-owned industrial enterprises number only about 4 million out of a Polish population of about 39 million, and it would be hard to justify granting the state enterprise solely to this sub-group of the population. Moreover, because the value of enterprises varies so widely within the industrial sector, there would be large disparities in the value of the assets given to workers if the enterprises are simply turned over to the workers within each firm. Of course, it would be even less justifiable ethically to give a sizable proportion of ownership directly to the management, which constitutes a very small proportion of the overall work force within the firm.

There are also important efficiency reasons for not privatizing directly through worker ownership. Worker-managed firms, for example, find it hard to borrow from outside creditors, who know that the worker-owners might later decide simply to raise their wages rather than pay back the loans. For the same reason, worker-owned firms find it hard to raise equity from outside investors. These factors help to explain why worker-managed firms play such a modest role in the capitalist world, despite the fact that they not prohibited, and in some cases are actually favored by special tax treatment. Significantly less than 2 percent of the industrial work force in the United States is employed in enterprises where workers own even 20 percent of the shares of the firm, and almost no major industrial firm is majority owned by the workers.

For these economic and political reasons, privatization should proceed with dispatch, but in a way that creates ownership in addition to the incumbent workers and management. The need for rapid and broad-based privatization poses the greatest logistical challenge facing the Eastern European reforms. Although much is known about stabilizing an economy, and much is known about how to liberalize, there is not a precedent for a societywide privatization, which in Poland encompassed about 3,000 state industrial firms and around 8,000 state-owned firms in total (including those outside of industry). The contrast with the United Kingdom, the world's leading privatizer in the 1980s, is stark. The British, unlike the Poles, only had a few dozen firms to privatize. They therefore had the luxury to proceed methodically with each firm to be privatized.

In the British privatizations, leading merchant banks prepared careful valuations of each enterprise, in order to set an appropriate price for the sale of the state's shares. Then, typically, a long public relations campaign was undertaken to explain the specific privatization to the public, and to attract potential investors. In some cases the enterprise itself was restructured in preparation for the privatization. Then, after restructuring, valuation, and a public campaign, the firm was sold, typically through a public offering of shares. Within Eastern Europe, this approach has come to be called the "British model."

Using this approach, the Thatcher government succeeded in privatizing about fifty industrial firms during the past decade, or about five per year. If Poland were to proceed at that rate, it would take two millennia for the state sector to be completely privatized—a pace too slow even for the gradualists! Poland's reformers had to find a way to speed the approach. Nonetheless, the British approach held sway during the first year of reform in Poland. This was understandable, if highly regrettable. Dozens of leading British merchant banks journeyed to the Polish privatization ministry to peddle their wares. The standard opening was, "I know how to privatize your economy; I managed a privatization for the Thatcher government in the mid1980s!" In this way, the British model unwisely became the early favorite in Poland, as it did in Hungary. Not surprising, it proved expensive and time consuming, and basically inappropriate in the Polish context.

The adoption of the British method of privatization as the preferred model was a fateful mistake for Poland's government in 1990, but it was not the only one that was made in this area (see Berg, 1992, for a detailed discussion of Poland's privatization strategy in 1990 and 1991). Of equal significance was the strategic decision to make privatization a *voluntary* procedure for each enterprise, leaving each enterprise the option of remaining in legal limbo as a state-owned enterprise. The privatization law of July 1990 spelled out in detail the procedures and options for each enterprise (mainly based mainly on the British model), but it left the ultimate decision on when to privatize to the workers' councils, the management, and the ministries with (theoretical) oversight responsibility over the enterprise. The government retained the power under the law to force an enterprise to privatize, but it was clear from the statute that this power was to be held in reserve.

The idea of a voluntary approach to privatization was an unsatisfactory response to a very real issue: that the workers' councils in the enterprises were already exercising some of the authority of ownwership (without the responsibility), and therefore resisted having the enterprise privatized without their approval. The Polish government should have recognized that a more effective approach would have been to require privatization of all state-owned industrial firms, but then to compensate the workers for their "lost" property rights by giving them special privileges during the privatization process itself, such as the right to receive shares for free or for a low price. Rather than compensating the insiders in the privatization process, the Polish privatization authorities instead gave them effective veto power over the process, with a result that the entire program was excessively delayed in implementation.[2]

In the event, the Polish government proceeded with a trial program of public offerings along the British approach in the second half of 1990, after the passage of the privatization law. (For a more detailed discussion of the logistics of privatization in the first two years of reform, see Berg, 1992.) The first five public sales proved to be very expensive in terms of fees and technical advice and much slower than the Polish government had expected. Though the initial five sales were carried off successfully at the end of 1990, they left 2,995 or so industrial firms to go! And during the several-month period of preparing the first five firms, the wage pressures remained relentless throughout the state sector, while many workers' councils started to organize as pressure groups to demand worker management and worker ownership. The efforts on behalf of worker ownership were abetted by gurus of worker ownership in the United States, who came to Poland to advocate this new system, despite its minimal role in the U.S. industrial sector.

While the privatization process for large firms stalled, the privatization of small-scale firms (mainly retail outlets and other service establishments) proceeded with dispatch. Here the process was not held up by the need to get agreement with workers' councils, managers, and so on. The responsibility was given to local governments, which used a mix of auctions, leases, and (in effect) giveaways to workers to get the tens of thousands of small establishments into private hands. The process proceeded rapidly and successfully, with almost no control from the central government. It is estimated that about 40,000 shops were sold or leased in the first year of the reforms, and that by the end of the second year, 90 percent of Poland's retail outlets were in private hands—both through a process of privatization and through the establishment of hundreds of thousands of completely new private firms.

For medium-size firms, including industrial enterprises up to around 500 workers, the government began to encourage leases and buyouts by workers and managers, in a process that became known in Poland as "liquidation." The term is confusing, since the liquidation in this case is not an actual splitting up of the firm's assets, but rather a legal winding-up of the state enterprise, followed by a leasing of the assets to the existing work force. About 1,000 enterprises were privatized via liquidation during the first two years of privatization.

During 1990, several policymakers and advisors skeptical of British-style privatization suggested the need for an across-the-board approach to large-scale firms that would cut through the logistical and political problems. This group argued for a "mass privatization" program, in which hundreds or thousands of firms would be privatized at the same time. These ideas began to receive a serious hearing toward the end of 1990, when the luster began to fade from the British model. The key to the mass privatization proposals was to think about the privatization process as one of *transferring* ownership back to the private sector, rather than selling enterprises as in the traditional approach. By transferring shares at zero or low cost, it would be possible to avoid the time-consuming process of valuing the enterprise and preparing it for a public sale. It would also be possible to create a politically and ethically acceptable system for distributing the shares to general public.

The idea of distributing, rather than selling, shares to the public already had intellectual roots among the Polish reformers. Two leading economists, Jan Szomberg and Janus Lewandowski (1990) had already floated the idea in 1988 in a widely circulated paper. Lewandowski was later to become minister of privatization, and from that position a champion of free distribution of shares. Earlier, Milton Friedman had made a similar proposal for Israeli privatization, and at least one case of free distribution of shares had actually been implemented, in the privatization of state-owned enterprises in British Columbia. Nonetheless, there was initial skepticism about the basic concept, and an urgent need to fill in the operational details.

In mid-1990, several colleagues and I (see Sachs and Lipton, 1990) recommended the following strategy of mass privatization based on a free distribution of shares.[3] We suggested that Poland's government put its attention on the thousand or so largest industrial firms, specifically those with employment of 1,000 workers or more. This group of enterprises includes around three-fourths of the total capital and employment in state-owned industry. All of those firms, *en masse*, would first be converted into 100-percent treasury-owned joint stock companies. This changeover in legal

form—known as "corporatization" or "commercializa-
tion"—would have several immediate and practical effects.
The enterprises would now operate under the Polish commercial code. Enterprise managers would be subject to the
same dictates (regarding legal responsibilities, conflict of
interest, and the like) as in private firms. The workers'
council would cease to have legal authority to appoint managers, though it would continue as an advisory body within
the firm, in the West European manner. The ministry of
industry would also lose its existing prerogatives to manage
the enterprises. An initial board of directors would be appointed. Under the Polish privatization law adopted in July
1990, reflecting a perfectly acceptable compromise, two-
thirds of the board of every treasury-owned company
would be appointed by the government and one-third by
the workers within the enterprise. After privatization of the
firm, defined as the transfer or sale of more than 50 percent
of the shares to private owners, a second board would be
appointed by a straight vote in the shareholders' assembly.

As soon as the corporatization takes place, it would be
possible to create real owners, at least for a portion of the
shares. We proposed the following methods for doing this.
First, some of the shares would be distributed directly to
the work force within the firms for free. This was not only
politically necessary, but ethically and economically advisable as long as the proportion of share ownership is modest,
say between 10 and 20 percent. The share ownership would
give the workers a stake in the success of the factory, without giving away so much of the ownership to the workers
as to risk cutting the firm off from the capital markets in
the future. The privatization law called for the workers
being able to buy up to 20 percent of the shares at half price.
In our view, it would be vastly easier logistically simply to
transfer 10 percent of the share ownership to the workers
completely free of charge.

Another fraction of the shares would be given to house-holds. One effective way to do this, from the point of view of corporate governance, would be to provide households with shares in investment funds (or mutual funds) rather than in individual enterprises. The investment funds in turn would own the shares of the industrial enterprises. Impor-tantly, the investment funds would be *private* institutions, licensed to operate under a new financial code. Each house-hold would receive, in effect, an equity claim on a very small fraction of a very large number of industrial enter-prises. The investment funds would help to govern the industrial firms by appointing directors and monitoring the firms' performance. Of course, the households would be free to sell their fund shares on the market, and to buy shares of individual publicly traded companies. The invest-ment funds as well would be free to trade or sell the shares in their portfolios.

After much debate, the Polish government embraced the basic approach of privatization through investment funds in its so-called Mass Privatization Program (MPP), unveiled in the spring of 1991. Since that time, however, the proposal has faced some fairly rough political sailing, and was still being debated by the Polish parliament at the end of 1992. The scope of the MPP was limited to around 400 large enterprises. The basic proposal calls for the licensing of between ten and twenty private investment funds, each with Polish ownership but with international management contracts. Every participating industrial enterprise would have its shares divided initially among the funds. For each of the industrial enterprises, one of the investment funds would serve as a "lead" fund. The lead fund would have a plurality of share ownership, while the other funds would receive a much smaller stake. Under the specific plans worked out by the privatization ministry, ten funds would be created. Each fund would be the lead for 40 enterprises, and would have small stakes in the other 360 enterprises. For every industrial firm, the lead fund would receive 33 percent of the shares, and the other nine funds would each receive 3 percent of the shares. The lead fund would have the power to appoint most of the initial board of directors, and would be expected to be an "active investor," monitoring the performance of the enterprise.

A debate has ensued about the exact methods of forming the investment funds, their powers, the nature of share distribution to the public, and other logistical issues. Various claims were made, such as: the investment funds would become politicized; the funds would end up controlling too much of Polish industry; or that foreigners would end up running the economy. These criticisms do not stand up to scrutiny, as safeguards were included in the MPP on each of these issues, limiting the powers of the funds and bolstering the independence of the funds from any kind of political interference. Nonetheless, the debate over the MPP proposals has continued until the time of this writing.

Since the time of the first mass privatization proposals in Poland, several other countries have taken the initiative on novel approaches of mass privatization based on the free distribution of shares. Czechoslovakia became the first major country to privatize large enterprises using vouchers. In that country, special privatization vouchers were offered for sale to Czechoslovak citizens at a low price. Voucher owners could use the vouchers to bid for shares of state enterprises that were put up for auction. Voucher holders were entitled to use the vouchers to purchase shares of individual enterprises, or to invest the vouchers in investment funds that in turn could use the vouchers to buy shares of industrial firms. Similar projects of mass privatization were undertaken in Lithuania, Mongolia, and then at the end of 1992, in Russia.

Some form of mass privatization strategy—whether with vouchers as in Czechoslovakia, or with investment funds as in the Polish MPP—should finally be implemented in Poland. It would enable Poland to privatize hundreds, or thousands, of large firms in a single round. It would establish broad-based ownership of industry, and also a reasonable system of corporate governance in which financial intermediaries (investment funds, commercial banks, pension funds) help to govern the enterprises to make sure that they act in the interest of shareholders. It would accomplish these goals without having to go through the long, difficult, and expensive task of case-by-case privatization, a task that has already proven to be nearly impossible in the Polish setting.

In addition to the investment funds, equity ownership by other kinds of financial intermediaries should also be encouraged. One attractive possibility would be share ownership by commercial banks, as is practiced successfully in Germany and Japan but is generally prohibited in the United States. (For an analysis of the efficiency of commercial bank holdings of corporate equity in Germany, see Cable, 1985; in the case of Japan, see Hoshi, Kashyap, and Sharfstein, 1990.) Currently, commercial banks are holders of large amounts of enterprise debts, much of which is bad debt because of enterprise insolvency. The privatization ministry and the government should encourage a kind of bankruptcy procedure, in which the commercial banks convert their bad debts into equity claims on the enterprises. This would help to establish equity ownership in the banks while offering the enterprises a kind of Chapter 11 restructuring. As of 1992, the Polish government and the World Bank were at work on this kind of approach.[4]

Shares could also be distributed into new pension funds that would be created to take over some of the obligations of the state retirement system. Chile offers a model of moving from a centralized state retirement system to a decentralized private system. Poland could follow this approach, with the state contributing its equity in state enterprises to the initial capital of the new pension funds. (For a discussion of this approach, see Diamond, 1992.)

In addition to the debates over worker ownership, and over mass privatization versus British-style privatization, there has been an active, and rather misguided, debate over whether enterprises should be "restructured" before privatization. The idea is that enterprises should somehow be prepared for privatization, perhaps through a financial restructuring, or divestiture of assets, or reduction of work force. This argument seems to emanate again from the British approach, and from the argument of investment bankers that an enterprise will be more valuable in privatization if it is first restructured.

The problem, once again, is logistical and political. There is no way for the government to become actively involved in the restructuring of hundreds or (even dozens) of large enterprises. The ministry of industry is technically unequipped for the job, and more important, would be subject to political "capture" by the enterprises it set out to restructure. Each government-led restructuring would be the occasion for lobbying for extra credits, debt relief, tax breaks, and other ad hoc priviliges. The Polish government actually learned this lesson the hard way at the end of 1991, when an ambitious but short-lived minister of industry announced her intention to implement an industrial policy for firms that needed government help. All of a sudden, she was bombarded with an avalanche of demands for bailouts. Expectations were raised; workers engaged in strikes and work actions to get the government's attention; social demands increased; and soon enough, the minister had to back off from this grand conception.

Let me conclude this section with a disclaimer. Privatization will not by itself produce miracles. Many factories are still outmoded or so poorly structured as to be unsalvageable. Many managers are also too inexperienced or inept to handle the difficult restructuring tasks that lie ahead. Moreover, corporate governance in private firms is far from perfect. Investment funds, commercial banks, and pension funds are often lax in their own oversight. We know too well from the U.S. experience that managers of privatization firms can also bilk the owners of corporate funds through excessive salaries and absurdly generous severance allowances.

Nonetheless, privatization will be highly therapeutic, if not miraculous. It is vital to industrial wage restraint and a reasonably efficient and nonpoliticized restructuring of Poland's large industrial enterprises. Perhaps most important, it will prevent an ongoing struggle over who owns what, so that Poles can most appropriately put their attention to creating new wealth and economic prosperity in the future.

The Social Safety Net

As a socialist state, the ethos of social equality permeated the letter if not the spirit of Poland's government policy during the communist period. Overt wage inequalities were kept low, much lower than in market economies. Social services, such as medicine and education, were provided free of charge to the population, though of course on a rationed basis. Pension and disability benefits were extended widely, to include, for example, farmers as well as industrial employees. And the government maintained a commitment to full employment.

It appears that the social policy was real, if somewhat less glorious than in the official communist propaganda. Income inequality was higher than in the official statistics, because politically connected individuals had privileged access to commodities that were unavailable in the consumer market. Health care for the communist *nomenklatura* was vastly better than for the average population. And some unemployment existed, even though it was officially forbidden. Nonetheless, it appears that the system promoted a greater degree of income equality, social service coverage, and low unemployment than in most market economies. In essence, there was a rough equality based on enforced mediocrity, as we have already seen in table 1.7, which showed that Poland had a far more equal distribution of income than countries of comparable per capita GNP in Latin America, or than the advanced industrial economies.

This is an important starting point for understanding the fourth pillar of reform: the construction of a social safety net. The starting point for reform was broadly favorable, as many social services already existed. The society was not deeply riven between rich and poor, as in Latin America. The most urgent need was for improved and timely targeting of assistance, rather than for the creation of a new social security system in its entirety. Over the longer term, there are important reforms necessary to ensure a more efficient delivery of social services.

The key steps at the beginning were the following. First, in the interest of ending the hyperinflation, across-the-board subsidies on foodstuffs and other items were slashed. This meant that more targeted assistance was needed to compensate the most vulnerable groups in the population. The key step taken here was to keep the pension payments to the elderly at adequate levels.[5] Pension benefits were indexed to inflation, and a 1990 initiative on benefits ensured that benefits actually rose more rapidly than industrial wages. The result has been to protect the real consumption of pensioners, as evidenced by their food consumption.

The second key step was to put in place a system of unemployment compensation and labor exchanges. This is the one piece of the social safety net that had to be set up in its entirety. Unemployment benefits were established at the start of 1990, and in fact, the system was initially too generous. By the end of the first year, when unemployment reached 6.1 percent of the labor force, it became apparent that many of the unemployed were individuals that had never been in the labor force and in fact were not actively looking for work. At the same time, other recipients had unreported jobs in the gray or black market. Eligibility requirements were tightened up at the end of the year. The unemployment rate continued to rise fairly steadily until late 1992, when it at least temporarily leveled off at about 13 percent of the labor force. As mentioned earlier, many Polish labor economists believe that about one-third of the unemployed actually have some form of unreported gainful employment.

Social spending naturally became a rallying cry of most political forces in the newly democratic parliament, and there has been a significant shift of budgetary priorities toward social spending. Government transfers to social funds (mainly the social insurance fund) rose from 2.3 percent of GDP in 1989 to an estimated 4.7 percent of GDP in 1991 (see de Crombrugghe and Lipton, 1992, for details), and according to IMF projections, no less than 7.9 percent of GDP in 1992. Total spending of the three social funds (social insurance fund, social insurance fund for farmers, and state labor fund) rose from 10.9 percent of GDP in 1989 to 14.9 percent of GDP in 1991. It is surely not true that the poor and vulnerable have been left out in the cold in Poland's reform. The real issues facing Poland are not the levels of social expenditure in the central government budget, which have risen by several percent of GNP, but rather the efficient delivery of social services. It is widely held that the health care system, the pension system, and the educational system are poorly managed and ill-designed for a market economy. Moreover, some aspects of social support, such as disability spending, seem to be flagrantly abused. Poland has among the highest disability rates in Europe (as measured by the proportion of disabled in the adult population), and there is widespread suspicion that the system is mismanaged at the local level.

Poland's Future Growth in an International Perspective

If all of the reforms are put in place—if stabilization and liberalization hold; if privatization moves forward; and if the social safety net helps to maintain overall social stability—what then are the growth prospects for a country like Poland? I would not pretend to give you an econometric estimate of Poland's future growth prospects. Any economist who promises to do so should think again. There is just no way to make precise estimates of growth, especially in Poland's current state of flux. In broad contours, however, we do know quite a bit about growth and what Poland's prospects are in the medium term. International experience indicates strongly that when poor countries open to the outside world on the basis of private ownership and free trade, they tend to *converge* with the wealthier countries, especially with the wealthier countries in their own neighborhood. That is, the poor country grow faster than the rich countries and thereby narrow the gap in living standards.

The postwar experience in Western Europe provides a strong demonstration of the powers of economic convergence. Table 3.1 illustrates this trend toward convergence in per capita income in almost all of the poorer countries of Western Europe: Portugal, Greece (which had strong convergence until 1980), Spain, and Italy (the single exception is Ireland, which did not narrow the gap in per capita

Table 3.1
Convergence of per capita GDP in Western Europe, 1955–1985

Ranking of countries from poorest to richest in 1955	Relative per capita GDP, 1955 (PPP basis)	Relative per capita GDP, 1985 (PPP basis)
Portugal	0.33	0.43
Greece	0.33	0.51
Spain	0.61	0.74
Ireland	0.64	0.60
Italy	0.69	0.85
Austria	0.84	1.02
Finland	0.96	1.05
France	1.01	1.14
Belgium	1.11	1.11
Germany	1.12	1.23
Netherlands	1.12	1.04
Iceland	1.21	1.03
Norway	1.22	1.45
Denmark	1.22	1.25
Sweden	1.23	1.13
United Kingdom	1.26	0.99
Switzerland	1.63	1.22
Unweighted average	1.00	1.00
Variance	0.157	0.071

Source: Heston and Summers (1988) data on per capita GNP, purchasing power parity basis.

income levels). Poorer countries and regions within Western Europe have tended to grow more rapidly than the richer countries and regions during the last forty years, thus narrowing the gap in living standards. Spain, as noted in the first lecture, is an important case in point for Poland, since the two countries started out at the same economic level in the mid-1950s. Spain began its strategy of opening up to Western Europe at the end of the 1950s. Thirty-five years later, Spain outstrips Poland in per capita GDP by four times!

The process of convergence is not guaranteed. Even with open borders, open trade, and membership in the European Community, growth can suffer disastrously as the result of

destabilizing macroeconomic policies. The experience of
Greece in the 1980s provides a sad testimony of what popu-
lism can do to a country that is a full member of the
European Community. The economic mismanagement of
Greece under Socialist Prime Minister Andreas Papandreou
destroyed economic growth and left Greece with a painful
macroeconomic legacy that will take years to overcome.

Some observers have worried that Eastern Europe might
be too peripheral to benefit from the market pull that aided
Spain, Portugal, and other countries. Are Poland and the
other Eastern European countries simply too distant from
the economic heartland of Europe to benefit from the basic
forces of economic integration? Economic geographers offer
us a way of answering this question. They have constructed
indicators of "economic distance" in which we measure
how far each country is from the economic center of gravity
of Western Europe. Table 3.2 presents the economic geogra-
pher's measure of economic distance between Poland and
the Western European market. As we see from the table,
Poland is in fact closer than Spain to the economic center
of gravity of Europe. The core of the Western European
market is in the industrial belt that extends from Brussels
to Stuttgart, and Poland is closer to that belt than is Spain.
Prague, of course, being west of Vienna, is even closer than
Warsaw to the industrial heartland. An economic geogra-
pher would argue that this helps to explain why Czechoslovakia was more industrialized than Poland in the prewar
period.

In sum, there is absolutely no geographical problem with
Poland's economic integration with Western Europe. Indeed, we should also note that transport costs between
Poland and Western Europe are very low.[6] Poland and
Northern Germany lie on a long, flat plain, making trucking
and rail transport easy and inexpensive. Poland's Baltic Sea
ports also link Poland to Scandinavia and to the Western

Table 3.2
Geographic accessibility of Poland and Spain to Western European market (EC and EFTA)

Index of accessibility of country i (higher value signifies increased accessibility).

With own market excluded:
Poland   7.44
Spain   6.19

With own market included:
Poland   8.68
Spain   10.31

	Distance (air miles) from:		
	Poland	Spain	GNP (1988, $bl)
Austria	342	1,124	126.9
Belgium	714	818	152.7
Denmark	415	1,280	107.7
Finland	585	1,835	104.7
France	844	653	950.0
Germany	557	885	1,208.3
Greece	995	1,470	52.5
Ireland	1,137	904	32.5
Italy	821	837	829.0
Luxembourg	676	807	6.7
Netherlands	686	908	227.6
Norway	666	1,476	91.2
Poland	65[a]	1,414	65.1
Portugal	1,771	319	41.8
Spain	1,414	134[a]	339.0
Sweden	532	1,619	178.6
Switzerland	642	772	183.7
United Kingdom	913	764	826.3

a. The "distance" to the own country is is calculated as $(1/3)*(sqrt(A)/\pi)$, where A is the area of the country in mi^2.
Source: Distances Dij between countries i and j are calculated as the straight distance between major cities. For all countries except Germany and Switzerland, capital cities are used. For Germany, Frankfurt is used, and for Switzerland, Zurich.

European ports on the North Sea. Poland's geographical advantage will become even more notable if Russia becomes an important market.

How fast can Poland grow in the 1990s? Spain and Portugal managed growth rates of around 5 percent in the first five years (1986–90) after membership in the European Community. Even before that, the promise of membership, combined with the progressive opening of the economies, led to strong growth in domestic and foreign investment. Poland should similarly be able to achieve at least this level of growth. In fact, given the backlog of technological and managerial improvements that can now be implemented in Poland, there are good reasons to expect that economic growth could reach 6–8 percent per year. One key, of course, will be for Poland to keep its public savings rate high (and therefore its budget deficit low) in order that the public sector contribute to the overall rate of capital accumulation in the country.

Some observers have suggested that Poland could hope to achieve "super-fast" growth rates, on the order of 8–10 percent per year, by following some of the economic prescriptions of the fast-growing countries of East Asia, especially the so-called Four Tigers—Hong Kong, Singapore, Taiwan, and South Korea. Are there important lessons from these countries that could be adopted in Poland to speed the process of convergence? In particular, is there a special formula of "industrial policy" in these countries that could be adopted to achieve super-fast growth?

I am unpersuaded by the argument that Poland should search for an "East Asian" industrial policy as the key to super-fast growth. There are several reasons for this. Most important, the industrial policies of the Four Tigers themselves vary widely. Hong Kong has had almost no industrial policy whatsoever, while Singapore's industrial policy has been both moderate and without apparent success, at least in comparison with laissez-faire Hong Kong.[7] Taiwan and Korea have employed much more industrial planning than Hong Kong and Singapore, but again of a very different variety. Korea has promoted very large industrial groups, while Taiwan's development has depended on small, family businesses. Second, those industrial policies that do exist in Korean and Taiwan were designed mainly to build up basic industries (e.g., steel, chemicals), while the task in Eastern Europe is one of cutting back in these sectors. Another point is that Korea can no longer get away with the kinds of managed trade policies that were purportedly elements of its success in the past. Korea finds itself facing very vociferous American and European criticism for continuing to protect markets, and so Korea is liberalizing rapidly under this international pressure. For Eastern Europe to even contemplate such a protectionist path would undermine their case for quick accession to the European Community. If they flirt with protectionist trade policies, the Eastern European countries will surely be hit with worse than they give by their trading partners in Western Europe!

This is not to say that Eastern Europe cannot learn much from the experience in East Asia. In my understanding, the real East Asian sources of high growth result from certain fundamental features of the economy, and not from a clever application of trade or industrial policy. The countries are huge savers, with savings rates of more than 30 percent of GNP. Macroeconomic stability is a hallmark of policy in all countries. Hong Kong does not even have a central bank that can engage in inflationary finance. The countries manage monetary and fiscal policies to maintain low inflation, budget equilibrium, and high savings rates. All of the countries have let the private sector be the engine of growth. The share of state enterprise is modest and declining in all of the countries. All countries have a rather equal income distribution, and therefore have been able to avoid high levels of internal social strife.One of the most hopeful aspects of the Eastern European political economy for the future is that the wealth and income distribution will also be rather equal, since the starting point is one of equality. As we have seen, communism succeeded in establishing equality in a perverse way—it left everybody poor!

The Role of the West

The fifth pillar of reform—the support of the West—is of fundamental importance, because economic integration will require definite and sometimes politically challenging actions in the West. The West must help in several different ways. First, of course, the West serves a crucial function as a role model for the reforming countries of Eastern Europe. The Western countries, especially the European Community, must help in a very practical way to provide the legal, economic, political, financial, and administrative guideposts for a market economy and a parliamentary democracy. The concrete goal should be the formal integration of Poland and the other reforming countries of Eastern Europe into the European Community. Second, the West is crucial as a market and also as a source of technology. Real economic integration must be two-sided, with the West opening its markets to Poland just as Poland opens its markets to the West. Protectionism in Western Europe could undermine the economic logic of reform and eat away at the political and social consensus of the reform program.

Third, the West is also crucial in the first years of economic reform as a source of emergency financial and technical assistance. The purpose of aid is not to rebuild Poland, but rather to give Poland a realistic chance at a fresh start. Old debts must be reduced, and emergency financial help must be provided in an expeditious way in order that controversial reforms are put in place and have the time to take hold. An analogy to U.S. bankruptcy proceedings is apposite here. When an enterprise successfully works its way through a Chapter 11 bankruptcy in the United States, three things typically happen. First, the creditors are forced to desist from pressing their claims. This breathing space, or financial standstill, gives the debtor the chance to get back on its feet. Next, the debtor may be allowed to borrow fresh funds on a privileged basis (with the new creditors having higher priority than the old) to replenish working capital. Third, the old creditors are usually compelled to cut a deal with the debtor, in which they cancel part of their debt or convert part from debt to equity, to allow the debtor to emerge from bankruptcy with an opportunity for continued operations.

Poland similarly needed the chance for a fresh financial start, and after a difficult period of negotiations, the Western official creditors wisely agreed to make this possible. The initial steps came at the end of 1989, when the West acted expeditiously by granting Poland two emergency credits: an IMF standby loan and a $1 billion stabilization fund for the zloty. These credits were enormously important in helping the economic reform team convince the Polish government to go ahead with the reforms, and convince the Polish public that the reforms had a good chance of succeeding. At the same time, Poland took a very important unilateral action that was both controversial and necessary. It announced to its creditors that it simply would be unable to service the $45 billion or so accumulated debts of the old regime during the first stages of reform, and would only be able to service the debts in part later on. Poland therefore appealed for a combination of rescheduling (postponement) and permanent reduction of the debt burden.

The debt reduction negotiations with the official (government-to-government) creditors were long and arduous. Poland's case was strong, in that the overhang of old debt from the past regime was potentially crippling to the budget and to Poland's needs to attract new investment funds. Poland also reminded its major creditor, West Germany, that it too had been the recipient of creditor relief, when the Western allies after World War II granted West Germany a package of debt cancellation in a 1953 treaty. Germany's debt cancellation was a critical element in allowing Germany to rebuild after the devastation of World War II. Certainly Poland merited nothing less.

After considerable debate, the official creditors granted Poland significant debt reduction in a two-stage arrangement unveiled in the spring of 1991. In the first stage, Poland's debts to official creditors were reduced by 30 percent. In the second stage, to be carried out in 1994, Poland's debts will be reduced by an additional 20 percent, on the condition that Poland remain in compliance with the terms of its restructuring agreement with the IMF. This conditionality, linking *future* debt relief with compliance on IMF commitments, is an important factor inducing Poland (and especially its fractious parliament) to maintain its commitment to politically difficult reforms.

The debt reduction agenda remains unfulfilled, however, as the commercial bank creditors, which hold about $10 billion of claims on Poland, have yet to match the debt reduction granted by the official creditors. The problem is understandable but vexing nonetheless. In a normal bankruptcy proceeding, all creditors are generally required to make sacrifices to reach an overall debt restructuring. The law provides mechanisms to force recalcitrant creditors into the deal. In international negotiations, however, where there is no bankruptcy court, it is harder to compel all creditors to join in a restructuring deal. In the case of Poland, the commercial banks have so far resisted joining in the debt reduction deal entered into with the Paris Club, in the hope that the partial cancellation of official debt will lead to greater payments on the commercial bank debt. Negotiations between Poland and the commercial banks will continue in 1993.

The West's financial support—a stabilization fund, IMF and World Bank support, government-to-government loans, and two-stage debt reduction—has been enormously important for Poland's reforms in the early years. The main unfulfilled part of the Western agenda is the commitment to long-term integration of Poland into the Western economic and political system. The key here is a clear Western commitment to Poland's timely membership in the European Community. That is the ultimate prize for Poland—the goal that is providing a considerable amount of the motive force of the entire reform effort. Unfortunately for Poland, the need to secure the commitment for eventual membership has come at the same time that the EC is grappling with the difficult problems of internal integration of the existing members. The EC has been enmeshed in its own difficulties of constructing the single market in Project 1992, and in moving toward a unified monetary system and foreign policy under the heavily disputed Maastricht Treaty. There have been many in the Community who have felt that the problems of "deepening"—that is, closer integration among the existing members—should take precedence over "widening"—the admission of new countries into the European Community.

The "deepening" versus "widening" debate has been sterile, debilitating, and misguided. The EC will be seen to stand for little indeed if it does not stand for the unity of all of Europe in a system of democratic and market-based states. If the EC were really to turn away the Eastern European countries, the moral authority of the EC would be so undermined as to call into question the idea of further deepening within Western Europe itself.

This basic point seems to be gaining recognition among the EC countries. Already in 1992, the EC negotiated special Association Agreements with Czechoslovakia, Hungary, and Poland. The Association Agreements point the way toward eventual membership, even though they fall far short of committing the EC in this regard. At the Edinburgh Summit of the EC at the end of 1992, the Community seemed to move still closer to a commitment to the Eastern European countries that membership will be welcomed in the coming years. Nonetheless, it remains urgent that the EC begin to negotiate a multiyear timetable with the Eastern European countries that explicitly leads to full membership of the Eastern European countries upon the substantial completion of the reform process.

Reform Prospects in the Rest of Eastern Europe and the Former Soviet Union

Three years after Eastern Europe's revolution, the comparative economic and political prospects in the postcommunist world are becoming a little more clear. Poland's economic reforms were of course highly controversial at the start of 1990. Now they are taken in general terms as a role model for much of the rest of the region. The experience of industrial collapse throughout Eastern Europe and the former Soviet Union has also clarified one key aspect of the reform process. Poland's steep fall in industrial production was not the result of a flawed reform strategy, but rather the result of the deep structural imbalances of its socialist economy—imbalances that are characteristic of the entire region. Thus the decline of heavy industry is occurring everywhere, whether reforms are fast or slow, coherent or incoherent. This was plainly evident in table 2.7, where we saw that Poland's decline of industrial production from 1989 to 1992 was in fact the *smallest* in the region.

With three years of perspective, we can now see that Poland has perhaps the best medium-term possibilities of all of the reforming countries. It has gone furthest in most areas of reform, both in comprehensiveness and in the speed of dismantling the old system (though, notably, Czechoslovakia went faster in implementing a program of mass privatization). This has meant that Poland is also first to start its economic revival, registering industrial growth in 1992 while Hungary, the Czech and Slovak Republic, and the rest of the region continued to experience decline. By virtue of nearly ten years of economic and political upheaval, Poland is probably also the most effervescent and dynamic of the countries in the political, economic, and social spheres, and probably for that reason, displays the most dynamic growth of the private sector.

Although Poland is ahead in reforms and in results, there are good reasons to believe that the reforms will prove successful in most of Eastern Europe, and most surely in the more Western parts of the region. Hungary, the Czech Republic, and Slovenia are all rapidly developing strong economic linkages with Western Europe. Exports to the West are growing strongly, and overall economic integration is taking hold. Deep social and economic linkages that were sundered a half century ago are being reestablished. The problems are more difficult the farther East one travels. Geography influences the depth of integration, so that Poland, Hungary, and the Czech Republic so far have much more extensive ties to Western European markets than do the Slovak Republic, Bulgaria, and Romania. Geography is also a critical factor in the historical character of the legal systems of the various countries, which were affected differently by the reach of Roman law, religious tradition, and domination of the more eastern countries (Romania, Bulgaria, Serbia) by the Ottoman Empire until the late nineteenth and early twentieth centuries.

The greatest issue for the region, and perhaps for world peace, is the prospect for economic and political reform in the former Soviet Union. Almost immediately after the collapse of communism and the end of the Soviet state, Russia embarked on a program of radical economic reforms rather similar to Poland's. There must be no mistaking the vastly more difficult conditions facing Russia's reformers, in scale of the country, historical experience, legacy of communism, and social and ethnic complexity. Russia covers nearly one-sixth of the world's land surface and eleven time zones, and is home to more than one hundred distinct national groups among its population of 150 million people. Its historical traditions have been partly Western and partly Asian, and often far removed from the mainstream of Europe. Roman law never extended to Russia, and the political system has been characterized by centuries of absolutism and a little more than one year of nascent democracy.

Nonetheless, as my colleagues and I have described elsewhere (Aslund, 1992, and Lipton and Sachs, 1992), the possibilities for successful economic reform in Russia are *much* better than typically believed, especially if Russia can successfully traverse the first few critical years of reform. Russian society broadly accepts the need for fundamental economic changes leading to a market economy. There are widespread signs of entrepreneurship and market activity even in the first year of radical economic reform. Commercial life is taking hold throughout the country, even though much of the new activity is not yet picked up by official statistics. Perhaps the greatest threat to reform is not the reaction of the Russian people, or Russia's long-standing social institutions, but rather the continuing political power of key groups from the old regime. In particular, the representatives of the military-industrial complex have remained a potent lobbying group for special credits and other kinds of government largesse. Their success in defending their old interests translated during 1992 into remarkably large subsidies for Russian heavy industry, in a torrent of credits of hyperinflationary dimension. Russia therefore entered 1993 on the brink of hyperinflation, hovering between financial chaos and successful reform. Successful reform will depend on further democratization and the emergence of new political groups that can compete effectively with the old military-industrial complex.

Poland's Remaining Tasks

Poland has made decisive and irreversible progress on constructing a market economy in the three years since the start of its reforms. While the economy remains in crisis, the possibility of continued economic improvement looks good. In my closing remarks, I would like to focus on the tasks remaining before Poland's reformers, to separate the urgent agenda from the long-term work of Poland's reconstruction and growth.

We have seen that enormous progress has been made on economic stabilization and liberalization. The economy operates overwhelming on a market basis. Price controls and trade controls are almost all eliminated. The risk of future hyperinflation seems to have been substantially reduced, if not completely eliminated. Nonetheless, the process of fiscal reform remains pressing. Budget deficits projected for 1993 and beyond of between 5 and 10 percent of GDP suggest the need for continued consolidation of the new market-based tax system, and the continued need for resisting pressures for unaffordable increases in social expenditures. Lower deficits and higher public-sector saving are needed to promote a higher rate of capital formation in the country, an important basis for higher economic growth. In addition, the government has work to do in the area of extending the government bond market, so that the deficits that remain can be financed through borrowing from Polish households and firms, rather than by money creation at the Polish central bank.

De Crombrugghe and Lipton (1992) have sketched out plausible long-term fiscal targets for Poland, shown in table 3.3, that would support macroeconomic stability and higher economic growth. The idea is to raise public revenues by a few percent of GNP, both to cover some further increase in social spending compared with the highly restricted spending of 1991, and to increase public investment spending signficantly, from 1.9 percent of GDP in 1991 to around 6 percent of GDP. Government saving would rise by 4.5 percent of GDP, comparing 1991 and the target levels. A "long-term" deficit of around 3 percent of GDP would be covered mostly by domestic bond issues and foreign financing, with domestic monetary financing held to around 1 percent of GDP.

The social safety net has been maintained and extended in crucial areas (especially unemployment compensation), and yet there is still great and justifiable unhappiness with the efficiency of government social services. The issues for the future in this area are less about the total amounts of funding than about the methods of delivery of services. The pension system should be privatized, at least in part, along the lines of the system in Chile. Abuse of the disability system and other social benefits should be reduced. There is a great need for restructuring of health and education to allow more choice and market orientation.

Table 3.3
Budget aggregates, 1991 and target (percent of GDP)

	1991	Target budget
Revenues	23.4	30.0
Current spending	24.9	27.0
Government saving	−1.5	3.0
Investment	1.9	6.0
Surplus (deficit (−))	−3.3	−3.0

Source: de Crombrugghe and Lipton (1992).

Privatization is another key item that remains on the policy agenda. Of course, "bottom up" privatization—the formation of new Polish firms—has proceeded rapidly, indeed more rapidly than almost anybody had envisioned at the start of the reform program. At the end of 1992, it is estimated that more than 50 percent of GDP, and around 60 percent of employment, is now in the private sector. And yet, the large industrial firms remain largely in state hands. It is therefore urgent to proceed with a mass privatization program, especially after three years of debate on the subject.

The last major economic step of enormous significance, in my view, is for the government to take additional measures to speed the process of integration with Western Europe. Of prime importance would be a concerted effort to attract foreign direct investment. Modern experience demonstrates that countries integrate economically with their neighbors not merely via international trade, but also via cross-country networks of production. Multinational enterprises now undertake their production in several countries at the same time, so that a single product might well have components produced in a dozen or more countries. Poorer nations aiming to catch up with the richer countries can speed the process by becoming part of the global production network, a pattern clearly evident in Mexico's increased production linkages with the United States, and in the East Asian Tigers' ever-closer production network with Japan.[8] To attract foreign investment, Poland should make sure that its investment procedures are streamlined, and that its physical infrastructure (transport, communications) is up-to-date and capable of supporting a dramatic growth in trade.

Perhaps the remaining key step to consolidating the economic reforms lies not in economics, but in politics. Poland's democracy remains fragile, not only because of the stresses caused by the turmoil of recent years, but also because of the inadequacy of Poland's existing constitution (inherited from the old system), and the inadequacies in some of Poland's approaches to democratic practice. Poland has, without question, one of the deepest democratic traditions of any country in the world. Its written constitution of 1791, just before the final partition, was the first in Europe. And yet the effective practice of democracy has eluded the Poles throughout history.

Poland first came to the attention of political theorists, especially Montesquieu, for its peculiar tradition of *liberum veto*. According to this tradition of the *Szlachta Sjem* (the nobles' parliament of the seventeenth and eighteenth centuries), any nobleman could frustrate an action of the parliament by a personal objection; all decisions had to be taken without even a single objection. Of course the system was unworkable. It succeeded in weakening monarchical despotism, as the Polish king was the weakest in Europe. But it also prevented effective collective action, such as raising an army to defend Poland against the encroachments of the neighboring empires. It was certainly a factor in Poland's complete dismemberment at the end of the eighteenth century.

The tradition of fractious parliaments and weak executives reemerged in the early years of the Polish democracy after 1918. Poland adopted an electoral law of proportional representation, guaranteeing the presence of very large numbers of very tiny parties in the parliament. There were thirty-one parties elected to the Polish parliament in 1926. As in Szlachta Sjem, Poland's post–World War I parliament proved incapable of dealing with the newly reestablished country's myriad problems. Marshall Pilsudski launched a nearly bloodless coup against the parliament in 1926, effectively ending Poland's democratic revival (though certain democratic norms survived until the communist period).

Ironically, despite this history, Poland once again opted for an electoral framework in 1991 of proportional representation, thereby again condemning the country to the possibility of paralysis in the face of a heavily divided parliament filled with tiny parties. The parliamentary elections that year, the first fully free elections since 1926, once again brought to the parliament a plethora of parties, this time twenty-nine. As a result, Poland's governments have been fragile multiparty coalitions. Combined with continuing strictures on executive authority (both the president's and the prime minister's), the result has been a continued risk of parliamentary paralysis and weak executive power.

It is urgent, in light of this history and recent experience, to put the political system on firmer ground through a series of constitutional and electoral changes. In my view, a new constitution should grant more authority to the Polish president, in a mixed presidential-parliamentary system, as in France. At the same time, the election law should be changed from a nearly pure proportionalism to a system in which parties must receive a threshhold of national votes, perhaps 5 percent, to win seating in the parliament. The threshold would limit the number of parties entering the parliament and thereby strengthen the larger parties. It would lead, as in Germany and elsewhere, to coalition governments with fewer parties and more stability.

The Historic Opportunity for Poland and the World

Looking back on Poland's history, one cannot help but be moved by the unique opportunity now before the country. This is the first time that Poland has had the chance to live in peace and prosperity with its neighbors, and with domestic freedom at home. Two centuries ago, Poland was dismembered. One hundred twenty-five years later, Poland reappeared as a sovereign nation, but in the midst of an unstable and violent Europe. The interwar period was spent grappling with hyperinflation, a trade war with Germany, the Great Depression, and finally the rise of fascism. Poland was destroyed more thoroughly than any other European country in World War II. Then it was brutally repressed by the Soviet Union for the next forty-five years.

Every time the Poles have been granted the opportunity they have accomplished marvelous things. Poland gave Europe the first written constitution in 1791. During the interwar period, against great odds, Poland successfully constructed the framework of a modern state. It even began to grow in the 1930s, in the midst of the worldwide Great Depression. And it gave the world Solidarity, which ushered in the democratic and peaceful revolutions of 1989.

The Poles show every evidence of displaying the same valor, energy, and skill that they have in the past, but now with even more favorable international circumstances. I believe that we will see great things from the Polish nation in the years ahead, as from many of the other long-suppressed peoples of Eastern Europe and the former Soviet Union. The world will benefit enormously from the creativity and talents of the region, and from the opportunity of a Europe united in democracy and market economy. It just remains for the West to help the East seize this historic chance, the best we have ever had to usher in an era of freedom and prosperity.

Notes

1. What Is To Be Done NOW?

1. Two years after the lectures, a newly elected Swedish government was equally explicit in the desire to harmonize with the European Community, and in fact to drop the notion of a separate "Swedish model" of the welfare state.

2. Using data on per capita GNP adjusted for purchasing power from the World Bank (1991, Table 30, 262–263), Portugal had about 50 percent of the EC income level in 1985, on the eve of accession to the EC. According to the same data, Poland had 37 percent of EC purchasing power in 1989 (note that the EC included ten countries in 1985 and twelve countries in 1989). Poland therefore has to grow 35 percent *more* than the EC to stand in the same relative position as Portugal in 1985, at half the EC average. If we take a leap of faith (as the data are not available) and say that in 1992 Poland also stood at 37 percent of the EC average, it would have to gain 35 percent in 8 years (between 1992 and 2000), or 3.8 percent per year. If the EC is growing at 2.5 percent per year, Poland would have to grow at 6.4 percent per year.

3. We see, however, that although school enrollment is very high at the primary and secondary levels, it is not high at the tertiary level. Full transformation of the society will involve a shift of emphasis and resources toward higher-level education as a necessary grounding for accumulating the human capital of the advanced industrial democracies.

4. For a comprehensive and authoritative analysis of the structure of socialist economies, see Kornai's (1992) masterful *The Socialist System.*

5. The standard joke about the chronic shortages of consumer durables and services revolves around the man who saves his money for years to purchase a car. After the man puts his bushels of zlotys across the table of the automobile bureau, the clerk tells him that the car will arrive ten years from today. The man calmly asks, "Is that morning or afternoon?" Incredulous, the clerk says, "Didn't you hear? I said ten years from today. What difference could it possibly make?" "Oh, it makes all the difference. The plumber is coming in the morning!"

6. The process of integration can be traced by membership in key European and international institutions. Spain joined the IMF in 1959; the OECD in 1962; and after a ten-year transition period agreed to in 1976, the EC in 1986. Poland joined the IMF in 1986, and remained part of the Soviet-dominated CMEA trading area until 1990. It 1992, it concluded a special Association Agreement with the EC, putting in motion a process that may culminate in EC membership in five to ten years. Poland has not yet become a member of the OECD.

2. Poland's Big Bang

1. The document was circulated to the Parliamentary Club of Solidarity, the OKP, in July (see Sachs and Lipton, 1989).

2. In the 1950s through the mid-1980s, the system was even less market oriented. Every exporter faced a distinct exchange rate at which it converted its foreign exchange earnings. Each importer also faced a distinct price from the central bank. There were in effect hundreds or thousands of exchange rates, and no active market in which exporters and importers were allowed to trade with each other directly.

3. Remember, when prices jumped at the start of the program, the existing money balances were no longer excessive relative to the needs for making transactions. Thus the situation changed from a monetary overhang (an excess supply of money) to a transitory monetary shortage, which was resolved in part by a conversion of household and enterprise dollars back into zlotys.

4. The stabilization fund was very important not only in calming the public and adding confidence to the currency, but also in helping Balcerowicz to convince sceptical policymakers to agree to the overall plan. Many policymakers doubted the possibility of achieving quick convertibility, partly because of their confusion about basic concepts. The availability of the $1 billion fund assuaged these fears and helped to generate a consensus behind the program throughout the government.

5. Remember from the first lecture that Polish real wages at the end of 1989 were unsustainably high, and that the rise in the real wage between 1987 and 1989 had not constituted an increase in real living standards. Similarly, the fall in real wages between 1989 and 1990 did not constitute a fall in real living standards.

6. Contrary to widespread misunderstanding, less than half of Poland's exports to the West in 1990 and 1991 were foodstuffs and raw materials. More than half of export earnings were in manufactures, with a diversified export base in chemicals, metallurgy, machinery, transport equipment, textiles, and clothing. The export boom after 1989 was centered almost entirely in manufactures, with sizable increases in earnings in most broad categories of manufactured commodities.

7. As the problem of shortages no longer existed after 1989, the official consumption data for 1990 and 1991 are more accurate than the official data for 1989. Nonetheless, there is still probably undercounting of consumption due to underrepresentation of purchases in the unregistered retail sector; undermeasurement of quality improvements; and a failure of the official data to capture the vast increase in the variety of consumer goods available in Poland.

8. Much better, 19 percent of respondents; a little better, 38 percent; much the same, 25 percent; a little worse, 15 percent; a lot worse, 3 percent.

3. The Return to Europe

1. The official data report that around one-third of enterprises are loss makers. Official statements, however, have acknowledged that the more accurate proportion is two-thirds. Unofficially, some leading Chinese policymakers have acknowledged that the true proportion of loss makers may be even higher than two-thirds.

2. The government also introduced some modest inducements for workers, but it was a case of "too little, too late." Under the laws, workers were given the opportunity to buy up to 20 percent of the shares of the firm at half of the market price. However, because "market price" could only be determined in the context of an actual privatization, the vast majority of workers had to wait for years until their firms were included in the trickle of British-style privatizations in order for their share privileges to be activated.

3. Several others advocated similar programs of mass privatization based on free distribution, including Aslund (1990), Frydman and Rapaczynski (1991), and Blanchard, et al. (1991).

4. There are several interrelated steps that are required. The banks themselves, to the extent that they are state owned, should be on a path of privatization. Bank regulations should give appropriate incentives to the banks to enter into the debt-equity conversion. The banks should be prepared technically to manage their new equity claims. And after the debt-equity conversions are carried out, many of the banks will require a new infusion of capital in order to maintain their positive net worth.

5. The elderly were also vulnerable because the high inflation of 1989 and 1990 had greatly reduced the real value of their monetary savings.

6. Of course, the "advantage" of low transport costs might be judged ironic, since it is also these low transport costs and absence of natural barriers that have helped make Poland the victim of countless invasions in the past centuries.

7. According to some analysts, indeed, Singapore's forays into industrial policy have been quite costly. See Allyn Young (1992).

8. It is estimated that around 40 percent of Mexico's trade with the United States is actually *within* enterprises operating both in Mexico and the United States, and shipping parts and finished goods between branches of the same firm.

References

Ammeter-Inquirer (1992). "Poland: Results of a Survey of Economic and Political Behaviour." Studies in Public Policy No. 201. University of Strathclyde. Glasgow: Centre for the Study of Public Policy.

Åslund, Anders (1992). "Prospects for a Successful Change of Economic System in Russia." Forthcoming in *The Transition in Eastern Europe*, edited by Olivier Blanchard, Kenneth Froot, and Jeffrey Sachs. Cambridge and Chicago: National Bureau of Economic Research and University of Chicago Press.

Berg, Andrew (1992). "The Logistics of Privatization in Poland." Forthcoming in *The Transition in Eastern Europe*, edited by Olivier Blanchard, Kenneth Froot, and Jeffrey Sachs. Cambridge and Chicago: National Bureau of Economic Research and University of Chicago Press.

Berg, Andrew, and O. J. Blanchard (1992). "Stabilization and Transition; Poland 1990–1991." Forthcoming in *The Transition in Eastern Europe*, edited by Olivier Blanchard, Kenneth Froot, and Jeffrey Sachs. Cambridge and Chicago: National Bureau of Economic Research and University of Chicago Press.

Berg, Andrew, and J. Sachs (1992). "Structural Adjustment and International Trade in Eastern Europe: The Case of Poland." *Economic Policy* 14, p. 117–173.

Blanchard, Olivier, R. Dornbusch, P. Krugman, R. Layard, and L. Summers (1991). *Reform in Eastern Europe.* Cambridge: MIT Press.

Cable, John (1985). "Capital Market Information and Industrial Performance: The Role of West German Banks." *Economic Journal* 95, pp. 118–132.

Chirot, Daniel, ed. (1989). *The Origins of Backwardness in Eastern Europe.* Berkeley: University of California Press.

Dahrendorf, Ralf (1990). *Reflections on the Revolution in Europe.* London: Chatto.

Davies, Norman (1984). *Heart of Europe: A Short History of Poland.* Oxford: Oxford University Press.

de Crombrugghe, Alain, and D. Lipton (1992). "The Government Budget and the Economic Transformation of Poland." Forthcoming in *The Transition in Eastern Europe,* edited by Olivier Blanchard, Kenneth Froot, and Jeffrey Sachs. Cambridge and Chicago: National Bureau of Economic Research and University of Chicago Press.

de la Dehesa, Guillermo (1993). "Political and Economic Reform in Contemporary Spain." Presentation to Conference on The Political Economy of Policy Reform, Institute of International Economic Studies, Washington, D.C., January.

Diamond, Peter (1992). "Pension Reform in a Transition Economy: Notes on Poland and Chile." Forthcoming in *The Transition in Eastern Europe,* edited by Olivier Blanchard, Kenneth Froot, and Jeffrey Sachs. Cambridge and Chicago: National Bureau of Economic Research and University of Chicago Press.

Economist (1990). *Book of Vital World Statistics.* New York: Random House.

Frydman, R., and A. Rapaczynski (1991). *Privatization and Control of State-Owned Enterprises,* edited by Ravi Ramamurti and R. Vernon. Washington, D.C.: World Bank.

Hoshi, Takeo, A. Kashyap, and D. Sharfstein (1990). "Bank Monitoring and Investment: Evidence from the Changing Structure of Japanese Corporate Banking Relationships." In *Asymmetric Information, Corporate Finance, and Investment,* edited by R. Glenn Hubbard. Chicago: University of Chicago Press.

Johnson, Simon (1992). "Private Business in Eastern Europe." Forthcoming in *The Transition in Eastern Europe,* edited by Olivier Blanchard, Kenneth Froot, and Jeffrey Sachs. Cambridge and Chicago: National Bureau of Economic Research and University of Chicago Press.

Korbonski, Andrzej (1992). "Poland: 1918–1990." In *The Columbia History of Eastern Europe in the Twentieth Century,* edited by Joseph Held. New York: Columbia University Press.

Kornai, Janos (1986). "The Hungarian Reform Process: Visions, Hopes, and Reality." *Journal of Economic Literature* 24, pp. 1687–1737.

Kornai, Janos (1990). *The Road to a Free Economy, Shifting from a Socialist System: The Example of Hungary.* New York: W.W. Norton and Company.

Kornai, Janos (1992). *The Socialist System: The Political Economy of Communism.* Princeton, N.J.: Princeton University Press.

Lenin, Vladimir (1902). *What Is to Be Done?* New York: International Publishers, 1969.

Lipton, David, and J. Sachs (1990). "Creating a Market Economy in Eastern Europe: The Case of Poland." *Brookings Papers on Economic Activity* 1:1990, pp. 75–133.

Lipton, David, and J. Sachs (1992). "Prospects for Russia's Economic Reforms." *Brookings Papers on Economic Activity* 2:1992, pp. 213–283.

Milanovic, Branko (1989). *Liberalization and Entrepreneurship: Dynamics of Reform in Socialism and Capitalism.* Armonk, N.Y.: M. E. Sharpe, Inc.

Roberts, Bryan (1992). "The J-Curve is a Gamma-Curve: Initial Welfare Consequences of Price Liberalization in Eastern Europe." Unpublished paper, MIT (July).

Rocznik Statystyczny, various issues, *Statistical Yearbook.* Warsaw: Central Statistical Office.

Rocznik Statystyczny Przemyslu, various issues, *Statistical Yearbook of Industry.* Warsaw: Central Statistical Office.

Rostowski, Jacek (1989). "The Decay of Socialism and the Growth of the Private Economy in Poland." *Soviet Studies* 41 (no.2), pp. 194–214.

Sachs, Jeffrey (1990). "Eastern Europe's Economies." *Economist*, January 13, 1990.

Sachs, Jeffrey (1992). "Accelerating Privatization in Eastern Europe: The Case of Poland." Proceedings of the World Bank Annual Conference on Development Economics 1991, Washington, D.C.: The World Bank, pp. 15–30.

Sachs, Jeffrey, and D. Lipton (1989). "Economic Program for Solidarity," July.

Sachs, Jeffrey, and D. Lipton (1990). "Privatization in Eastern Europe: The Case of Poland." *Brookings Papers on Economic Activity* 2:1990, pp. 293–341.

Szomberg, J., and J. Lewandowski (1990). "Property Reform as a Basis for Social and Economic Reform." *Communist Economies*.

Weitzman, Martin (1991). "Price Distortion and Shortage Deformation or What Happened to the Soap?" *American Economic Review* 81 (no. 3), pp. 401–414.

World Bank (1989). *Social Indicators of Development, 1989.* Baltimore: Johns Hopkins University Press.

World Bank (1990). *World Development Report, 1990.* Oxford: Oxford University Press.

Young, Allyn (1992). "A Tale of Two Cities: Factor Accumulation and Technical Change in Hong Kong and Singapore." *NBER Macroeconomics Annual, 1992.* Chicago: University of Chicago Press.

Index